SOUND ADVICE

music's effect on life, health and happiness

rick notter

Large-quantity purchases or custom editions of this book are available at a discount from the author. For more information, contact the author at 1-800-968-4606, or write to: Rick Notter, PO Box 7421, Bloomington, IN 47407, or send an email to Rick@ BetterSoundAdvice.com.

To make comments or suggestions, visit the Sound Advice website at: www.BetterSoundAdvice.com.

ISBN: 1-4392-0380-6
ISBN-13: 9781439203804

Library of Congress Control Number: 2008906517

"Sales teams need every advantage possible to gain a competitive edge. Rick's presentation of the research in *Sound Advice* brought the techniques to life for our sales team. Improving the team's mood and increasing their awareness on their health allows them to focus on motivating themselves, and each other. *Sound Advice* is good advice if you need to find the edge for your team."

- T. Edward Burke

Insurance Executive

& Sales Training Specialist

"I really enjoyed the statistics and the history behind the stories. I love that Rick does not tell me what to do, he tells me why to do it."

- Renee Casserly

Director of Business Development, Blue Shield of California

"The techniques on how to relax from *Sound Advice* helped me relieve the stress I was feeling recently and now my work day is more manageable. I recommend this to anyone who wants a little stress relief."

- Alan McDonald
Senior Director of Operations, Fox Sports Interactive

"As a professional dancer, I have always believed in the benefits of music and movement, and have seen the difference in the adults and kids I work with and how it transfers over into their daily lives, be it improved self-confidence, agility and strength, memorization, and even self-expression. Rick touches on each of these subjects with great references and ideas for application that anyone can enjoy."

- Lesha Montoya
CEO, ShutUpNDanceCompany.com

To my father, my family, and my friends.

TABLE OF CONTENTS

ACKNOWLEDGEMENTS

So many wonderful people contributed in some way to this project. I would like to thank all of them but especially the following:

Thanks to my wife, Mary, and children, Katie and Rich. They all inspire me in their own way every day. I've been blessed to be surrounded by such wonderful people.

Thanks my good friend, Terry, who encouraged me to write on a regular basis. Whenever we would see other authors and their presentations, he would always ask, "Why aren't we doing something like this?" Terry, I finally got around to it. Now it's your turn.

To my sister, Jackie. She is not only a talented dancer, singer, and salesperson; she is also a very good editor. Jackie did an excellent job of correcting the mistakes I made when writing this book.

To my friend and former co-worker, Renee. She pushed me many times to complete this project. I believe I met the deadline she set for me.

My good friend, Kevin, who inspired me to get finally this book to the printer. Kevin finished his project well ahead of me and continues to have success with it. It is a children's book called *Deputy Dorkface: How Stinkville Got Cleaned Up*. Look for it on Amazon.com.

To my late Aunt Lucille Notter. Her books on research in the field of nursing were pioneering and continue to get regular use to this day. When I was a child, seeing her name on her books gave me the desire to write a book of my own someday.

Thanks to all the authors referenced in this book who shared so much of their knowledge on music. Also to the researchers who continue to help us all learn more about the power of music. Don't stop now, there is still much we do not know.

Thanks to the musicians who compose and perform the songs that touch our hearts, minds, and souls.

Finally, thanks to all the music teachers around the world. They inspire so many and rarely receive the recognition they deserve.

Introduction

Ever wonder why music can be so soothing? What causes a song to be stuck in your head? How it can inspire you to dance or exercise? So have I. As the curious type, I set out to find out why this happens. I am not a doctor, psychologist, or even a professional musician. Just a person who loves music and has used music to help get through good times and bad in my life.

The idea for this book came about because of a tag line I started using in all my e-mails. After having gone through surgery for cancer and deciding my attitude would be the difference in beating this disease, my e-mails included the following lyrics from a song by The Eagles in my e-mail signature:

> *"So often times it happens that we live our lives in chains And we never even know we have the key."*
> – ***The Eagles, Already Gone***

This line, to me at least, is very profound. You will read more about why later in this book. The response I received to this simple tag line got me thinking. What other lyrics have I thought about in my life that had an effect on me? For that matter, why have I always used music when I had moments of solace, joy, or inspiration?

I remembered listening to Eric Clapton's *Running on Faith* when struggling through the first year of starting my own business. Singing the words to The Beatles *Help!* when I felt alone in life. Playing Van Morrison's *Bright Side of the Road* or Monty Python's *Always Look on the Bright Side of Life* whenever I needed a little cheering up.

I concluded that there was a certain enlightenment; a Zen, if you will, that I felt when listening to music and that Zen could help many other people live their life to the fullest. That started the book project that has now taken over two years to compile.

While I have not found complete answers to all the questions I went in search of, I do know that music can do so much to improve our lives. The books, research papers, news articles, and more that I have read in investigating this topic all point to music having more to offer than just notes played on musical instruments. I hope you will enjoy reading and using the information here as much as I did bringing it all together.

"There is something very wonderful in music. Words are wonderful enough; but music is even more wonderful. It speaks not to our thoughts as words do; it speaks straight to our hearts and spirits, to the very core and root of our souls. Music soothes us, stirs us up; it puts noble feelings in us; it melts us to tears; we know not how; – It is a language by itself, just as perfect, in its way, as speech, as words; just as divine, just as blessed."

– Charles Kingsley, English novelist

CHAPTER ONE – SOUND IDEAS
THE ZEN OF MUSIC

"Garbage In, Garbage Out" is a phrase from the world of computer science. It refers to the fact that if you input nonsensical data into a computer, it will produce a nonsensical output. The reverse is also true. The more accurate information you can provide, the more accurate the results the computer will generate.

For human beings, the brain is our computer – a processor that works very much in the same way. Garbage in will likely produce bad results and vice-versa. The difference between humans and computers is that we can control much of the input. Every day we make choices, thousands of them, about what we hear, see, smell, taste, and touch. The more positive the input, the greater the chance of a positive result.

What we have discovered over thousands of years, and we are just beginning to understand why, is that music can have a powerful effect on us in many ways. Our brains are wired for sound, musical sounds. When used in the right way, music is power.

The power to soothe. The power to inspire. The power to cure. A force found throughout the universe with the ability to penetrate to the deepest parts of our bodies and souls. A force found in every civilization, no matter how isolated, throughout history. A force that we can use daily to put us in a better mood, improve our health – even inspire us to change our lives.

How can you harness this force to your advantage? Well, the purpose of this book is to show you ways to use the power of music in your life. How utilizing that iPod of yours at key times can help you feel better, look better, and be better.

How do I know this will work for you? Personal experience for one. Music has helped me lose weight and stay positive through some very tough times in my life. More importantly, there are volumes of research to back up the information found in the following pages.

There are no startling revelations. Most of this has been published or reported on before. Instead, what I have done is compile all of this data into segments that you can use.

S O U N D   M A C H I N E

In each section, you will find a list of songs that go with the information presented. These songs are my personal preferences. You may like them. You may not. In either case, there are hundreds of songs that fit into these categories, so feel free to change the list to fit your personality. It does not matter, as long as you find tunes that help you accomplish your goal – exercise, relaxation, inspiration, or whatever.

Also included are excerpts from song lyrics that are appropriate for the subject matter. Again, personal preference, but I believe you will find that they fit well.

There are suggestions in here that may or may not apply to your life at this time. Odds are, however, all of it will apply at some time in your life.

You do not necessarily need an iPod, either – although I find the device to be one of the most convenient ways to listen to music. A CD player, cassette tape, or even an old vinyl record can all serve the same purpose.

If you do use an iPod, or any other device requiring the use of headphones, use caution with both the volume and the places you use it. High volume music played through headphones has been known to cause hearing loss. The use of headphones also takes away, temporarily, one of your five senses. Therefore, if you are running or biking outdoors, be aware you will not be able to hear traffic and other possible dangers as easily.

SOUND BEGINNINGS

"Music has charms to soothe the savage breast
To soften rocks, or bend a knotted oak."
– William Congreve, English dramatist

Some 300 years ago, those words opened the play, *The Mourning Bride*. Today, it is often misquoted as "Music can soothe the savage beast" thanks, in part, to a 1950 Bugs Bunny cartoon, *Hurdy-Gurdy Hare*, where Bugs calms a gorilla with music. Still, people have known for centuries that music can have a calming effect.

While much is known about the origins of man, very little is known about the origin of music. Archaeological digs have discovered musical instruments tens of thousands of years old. Recorded history shows evidence of composed music nearly four thousand years ago.

Yet, how did man discover music? Was it in the same way he discovered fire? The wheel? Or was it Divine inspiration?

Darwin put forth the theory that early man developed the ability to sing before he learned to speak as a way to charm members of the opposite sex. Others believe that mothers have soothed babies with soft, melodic singing for tens of thousands of years.

While no one knows for certain how man found music or if music found man, it is known that music and harmony have been a part of the universe for billions of years.

The Power of Music

Pythagoras first theorized that everything in the universe produces sounds and much of it is in harmony. You may remember Pythagoras (who lived around 500 BC) for the Pythagorean Theorem from geometry class. The theorem, where $A^2 + B^2 = C^2$ determines the area of a right triangle, was not discovered by Pythagoras, but he was able to prove it and popularized it in the Greek world.

Pythagoras did discover, however, that there was a connection between math and music. He found the intervals in notes could be expressed in mathematical terms – a ratio of 2:1 in the length of two strings to produce two different tones in an octave step. This laid the foundation of musical theory and teachings for centuries to come.

> *"If I were not a physicist, I would probably be a musician. I often think in music. I live my daydreams in music. I see my life in terms of music. ... I get most joy in life out of music."*
> – **Albert Einstein**[1]

Some 2200 years after Pythagoras put forth his theory on octaves, Wolfgang Amadeus Mozart began composing some of the most beautiful music ever created. It may also be some of the most powerful music.

There are those that believe that Mozart's music has the ability to treat diseases of the mind and body, and can enhance one's ability to learn. The Mozart Effect, as it is referred to, is subject to debate. There is no debate, however, that music can have positive effects on humans.

> *"Music is the one incorporeal entrance into the world of higher knowledge, which comprehends mankind, which mankind cannot comprehend."*
> – **Ludwig van Beethoven**

SONG STUCK IN MY HEAD

Within the past few decades, the amount of research done on music and its effects on humans has increased significantly. With few exceptions, the results have shown there is something special about the way our minds and bodies react to music.

The research runs the gamut – from how certain notes on a xylophone can destroy cancer cells (more on this later) to why we get a song stuck in our head (which can drive us crazy, especially if it is something we don't care for).

By the way, University of Cincinnati marketing professor James Kellaris calls this an "Earworm." Kellaris has studied the phenomenon of getting songs stuck in our heads since 2000[2]. He believes the more neurotic a person is the longer the Earworm is likely to reside in the head. Kellaris' theory on why it happens is that when you hear a portion of a song, the brain tries to complete it by filling in the missing information, which leads to "unsticking" the earworm.

Professor William Kelley of Dartmouth College went so far as to use brain scanning to find out what happens when we get an earworm[3]. The scans showed the brain actually filled in the gaps of familiar songs.

All of this research, even as trivial as studying earworms, goes a long way in determining why music has these effects on our minds, bodies, and emotions. It will also help find more ways to use music to its fullest potential.

"Music is not deception, but revelation. Its unique power is to reveal to us elements of beauty which are not accessible by other means, the contemplation of which reconciles us to our lives not just for the moment, but forever."
– Pyotr Tchaikovsky, Russian Composer

T H E M E   S O N G S

You have already witnessed the power music can have on some people when used as a theme song. President Bill Clinton was elected to his first term in office thanks, in part, to his playing the saxophone on *The Arsenio Hall Show* and by the decision his campaign staff made to play Fleetwood Mac's *Don't Stop* at campaign rallies.

Don't stop, thinking about tomorrow,
Don't stop, it'll soon be here,
It'll be, better than before,
Yesterday's gone, yesterday's gone.
   – Fleetwood Mac, Don't Stop

The old Sister Sledge tune *We Are Family* was the rallying cry of the 1979 Pittsburgh Pirates, who went on to win the World Series.

Every day, Ellen DeGeneres opens her show with music and dances with the audience to help get them in a better mood. Is it any wonder the show continues to get high ratings and is the only talk show in the history of the Daytime Emmy Awards to win three consecutive awards for Outstanding Talk Show in its first three seasons?

Even the lyrics of songs can make a difference, as shown in the movie *Dangerous Minds* – the real life story of a teacher who used Bob Dylan songs to inspire her students.

So put the power of music to use for you. Invest in an iPod or other portable music player (prices have come down quite a bit since the iPod was first introduced in October 2001) and download the tunes that could help change your life.

> *"There are thoughts and there are feelings that we have that there are no words for. That's where language ends and music takes over. Those feelings are very strong and they are enough to get us to jump to our feet and cheer."*[4]
> **– Michael McDonald**

Again, you will find suggested selections in the pages to follow, but there are hundreds of other songs that are just as appropriate. A lot will depend on your personal preferences.

For other selections, additional research, or links to more information on music, dancing, etc., visit my Web site at www.BetterSoundAdvice.com or www. ZenOfMusic.com.

Now, to quote REO Speedwagon, it's time to turn some pages and "Roll With The Changes."

THE ZEN TEN

What Music Can Do To Improve Your Life
(Each will be explained in the pages to follow)

1. Put You In A Better Mood
2. Help You Relax
3. Induce You To Exercise
4. Inspire You
5. Motivate You
6. Improve Your Memory
7. Help Your Health
8. Stir You To Dance
9. Assist You In Learning
10. Facilitate A Better Night's Sleep

Notes

There's a healing in those guitars
And a spirit in the song
No matter what condition your rhythm is in
The message goes on and on
Music is the doctor
Makes you feel like you want to
Listen to the doctor
Just like you ought to
Music is the doctor of my soul

*– **The Doobie Brothers, The Doctor***

MUSIC MAN M.D.

In the classic Broadway show *The Music Man*, the plot revolves around a con man who convinces a small Midwestern town to start a boys marching band to keep the youngsters "moral after school." The con man's plans go awry when he learns a lesson in morality from the local librarian. The feel good comedy was a hit on Broadway and later on the big screen.

I am not sure how much morality youngsters are learning from today's music (although there are plenty of inspiring lyrics we will get to later in this book), but I do know music can have some very powerful effects on healing and your health.

Music therapy is an established health profession that utilizes music, singing, and even dancing in the treatment of patients. While it is a relatively young profession – Michigan State University established the first degreed program in 1944 – it has roots that go back centuries.

More than 2500 years ago, mathematician Pythagoras taught his followers that music could help heal illness both mental and physical. A fine musician, he often played music for the sick and was reported to have spent months with a dying friend, playing the Lyre to help ease his pain.

Pythagoras believed that music and diet were key ingredients for living a long, healthy life. Incidentally, one of the foods he told people to avoid was beans, even declaring it a sin to eat them. Either he knew about the aromas beans could produce after digesting them or he was not quite prepared to explain the "musical fruit."

While there is no evidence to support the Pythagoras theory on beans, there is plenty of research to support the healing powers of music. The brain, heart, circulatory system, and even the skin can be positively affected by music.

Let's start with the effect music can have on the brain.

OF SOUND MIND

Anyone who grew up in the 70s and 80s is probably familiar with SchoolHouse Rock. The animated series was a staple of Saturday morning television on ABC. The Emmy-awarded winning cartoons taught a generation of kids more about multiplication, grammar, and U.S. government than many learned in the classroom. It was the concept of learning the ABC's through song but with material that is more complicated.

Conjunction Junction, what's your function?
Hooking up words and phrases and clauses.
Conjunction Junction, how's that function?
I got three favorite cars
That get most of my job done. Conjunction
Junction, what's their function?
I got "and", "but", and "or",
They'll get you pretty far.

– Conjunction Junction, SchoolHouse Rock

The idea got its start in a most unusual way. The chairman of a big New York ad agency, David McCall, was frustrated by the fact that his son could easily remember the lyrics to songs by The Rolling Stones and The Grateful Dead, but he could not get the knack of simple multiplication tables.

McCall enlisted his agency's creative staff and a Texas jazz musician named Bob Dorough to link music with math (Pythagoras would be proud), and the result was a catchy little tune called "Three Is a Magic Number."

The song was first released on an album of similar material called *Multiplication Rock*. Unfortunately, the records did not exactly fly off the shelves. Then, a member of the agency's creative staff, Tom Yohe, decided to add animation to the songs, creating some of the first music videos. The animated songs were shown to the folks at ABC, who decided to air them during its Saturday morning cartoons, and an educational institution was born. The series originally aired from 1973 to 1985. The cartoons still get some air time to this day and have been released on DVDs that get frequent use in classrooms across the country.

SchoolHouse Rock was successful because it capitalized on the combination of music and memory. Recite a written paragraph and it will be difficult for you to memorize. Sing it, however, and you may never forget it.

> *"Music is a more potent instrument than any other for education, because rhythm and harmony find their way into the inward places of the soul."*
> *– Plato*

How the brain combines music with memory is not completely understood, but science is getting a better grasp on how music affects the brain. While many body movements and senses can be tied directly to certain areas of the brain, music appears to be the ultimate stimulator – affecting several areas of the brain at the same time.

ALWAYS ON MY MIND

In *"This Is Your Brain on Music,"* neuroscientist Daniel Levitin explains how his research has discovered the unique ways music activates different areas of the brain. One area affected is the cerebellum, the base of the brain, which integrates sensory perception and motor output. This is where, according to Levitin, the brain synchronizes to the beat of the music.

This would help explain the entrainment effect on our body – where runners speed up or slow down to the beat of the music. It also explains how heart rhythms and blood pressure can change based on the music a person hears. Levitin goes on to explain how music has similar effects on emotion, pain, and pleasure.

The effect on memory is the most compelling. Somehow, the brain plays an association game. It matches words with sounds and stores them for later recall. This is why you can remember the words to a song you have not heard in 20 years, but you cannot recall the exact words in a conversation you had only 20 minutes ago.

This point was proven recently at Kansas State University, where researchers found people had extremely clear recollections tied to certain music.[5] After seeing just a song title or a few seconds of a song, participants in the study could use that as a cue to recall vivid memories.

This is not the only way memory is activated through association. You remember where you were when you heard about the assassination of President John F. Kennedy (for those old enough to remember this), the attacks on the World Trade Center, or when you learned Princess Diana died – all because of the association your brain has between the event, time, and place.

There is a scene from the classic 1967 movie, *The Dirty Dozen*, where the men remember the details of their assignments through a rhythmic rhyme, with each part of the mission corresponding to a number. It is a perfect example of memory through association.

- ✓ *One: down to the road block we've just begun*
- ✓ *Two: the guards are through*
- ✓ *Three: the Major's men are on a spree*
- ✓ *Four: Major and Wladislaw go through the door*
- ✓ *Five: Pinkley stays out in the drive*
- ✓ *Six: the Major gives the rope a fix*
- ✓ *Seven: Wladislaw throws the hook to heaven*
- ✓ *Eight: Jiminez has got a date*
- ✓ *Nine: the other guys go up the line*
- ✓ *Ten: Sawyer and Gilpin are in the pen*
- ✓ *Eleven: Posey guards points Five and Seven*
- ✓ *Twelve: Major and Wladislaw go down to the devil*
- ✓ *Thirteen: Franko goes up without being seen*
- ✓ *Fourteen: Zero hour, Jiminez cuts the cable Franko cuts the phone*

✓ *Fifteen: Franko goes in where the others have been*

✓ *Sixteen: we all come out like it's Halloween*

S O U N D   M E M O R Y

Music can take the depth of this memory to levels few knew existed. *The Man with the 7 Second Memory* is a remarkable story that illustrates this phenomenon. The British documentary profiles the life of Clive Wearing, a man whose memory was all but destroyed by a severe case of Encephalitis in 1985. The doctors were able to save Wearing's life, but he was left with a memory that can recall only what has happened in the last seven seconds. The one person he recognizes is his wife, Deborah. If you met Clive, left the room and came back 30 seconds later, he would not remember you.

What Clive Wearing can remember, however, is music. Once a renowned musician and conductor, he can recall how to play music. He just does not remember how he knows how to play. Wearing can play a song on the piano perfectly from beginning to end, sing completely in tune, and even conduct an entire orchestra. When he finishes, Clive forgets he has played and starts shaking – a result of his inability to control his emotions. Apparently, the brain is trying to process information to places that no longer exist.

While Clive Wearing's catastrophic memory loss is rare, there are comparisons between his condition and a severe case of Alzheimer's disease. In those cases, as well as cases of dementia and Parkinson's disease, music is the key to unlocking memories seemingly trapped forever by these conditions.

For a more recent example of this music-brain phenomenon, do a Google search on Derek Paravicini and watch the 60 Minutes report on this musical savant. His talent is amazing.

Patients will often respond to music when they respond to nothing else. It can be as simple as remembering the words to a song they sang as a child – *Ring Around The Rosy, Home On The Range, or Twinkle, Twinkle Little Star.* For Harvey Alter, featured in a *New York Times* story on melodic intonation therapy, it was the song *Happy Birthday* that helped him recover from a stroke.[6]

These are the cases where music therapists are often most effective. (If you know someone who suffers from Alzheimer's, Parkinson's, or schizophrenia, make sure part of his or her treatment involves music therapy.)

> *Memories, pressed between the pages of my mind*
> *Memories, sweetened thru the ages just like wine*
> *Quiet thought come floating down*
> *And settle softly to the ground*
> *Like golden autumn leaves around my feet*
> *I touched them and they burst apart with sweet memories,*
> *Sweet memories*
> **– Elvis Presley, Memories**

In late 2006, "Dilbert" cartoonist Scott Adams was stricken with a severe case of spasmodic dysphonia – a mysterious disease that causes the parts of the brain that control speech to shut down or malfunction. Adams could only speak if he pinched his nose or spoke in rhyme. While Adams did undergo several medical treatments, it was not until he began chanting the nursery rhyme "Jack Be Nimble" repeatedly that he was able to speak again somewhat normally. Reciting the nursery rhymes helped to "re-map" his brain and cure his speech issues.

Putting this music/memory science to work for you today can help you at work, in school, and at home. You can easily memorize lists, formulas, names, etc. by putting them to song or rhyme. This is one of the most basic memory improvement techniques. The more associations you can create with something the more likely you are to remember it when you need the information.

Have any doubts this might work? Read some of the lyrics in this book and think about how often that song immediately started playing in your head. The link between words and music can be very strong.

It might also help you to turn off the television. An Australian study found those who watch less than an hour of television a day performed better on all memory tasks than those who watch TV more often. The exception – TV quiz shows and news programs.[7]

S T R I K E   U P   T H E   B A N D

If you want to take memory improvement a step further, learn how to play music. Research has shown that the more musical training you have, the better your verbal memory will be. Studies of musicians have found that the brain has the capacity to change its wiring to support musical activities.[8] The research showed that areas of musicians' brains are hyper-developed as a result of musical training – and the younger they start playing, the more expansive this development is.

Work at the University of Heidelberg in Germany discovered that the auditory cortex of musicians was 130 percent larger than that of non-musicians. Additionally, more area of some musicians' brains is devoted to motor control of the fingers used to play an instrument. In violinists, sensory inputs for the four fingers used on the strings were much greater than those for the hand that had to focus just on moving the bow. Musicians who use both hands to play, such as pianists, show greater coordination between the motor regions of the two hemispheres of the brain. In addition, the anterior corpus callosum, which interconnects the two motor areas, is larger in musicians.

At Northwestern University, neuroscientists found concrete evidence that playing music enhances the brain and sharpens hearing for a variety of sounds, including speech.[9] These findings reinforced the importance of music classes in schools.

No matter what your age, your brain still has the ability to do some rewiring and respond to music lessons. Ideally, you want to start as early as you can. If you have children, start them in music lessons even before they start school.

Children who were exposed to music in their homes on a regular basis at a young age (under age five) had greater brain auditory activity than those three years older who did not have music in their homes.

In 2001, music students scored 11 percent higher on SAT tests than non-music students. Moreover, a Swiss study found students involved in the music program were better at foreign languages, learned how to read more easily, demonstrated more enjoyment in school, and had a lower stress level than non-music students.[10]

If efforts are being made to cut back on music education programs in your local schools, do everything you can to stop these cuts. If anything, music education should be a required course in elementary schools. The benefits are far too great for music to fall victim to the budget-cutting axe.

My wife, Mary, and I stressed music with both our children from a very young age, and we saw the positive effects it had. Both Katie and Rich played instruments through grade school and high school. Rich has a great appreciation for music and continues to play both guitar and the saxophone.

When something gets in my way I go round it.
Don't let life get me down
Gonna take life the way that I found it.
I got the music in me
I got the music in me
   – The Kiki Dee Band, I've Got The Music In Me

SOUL MUSIC

Music's positive effects go well beyond the mind and memory. Studies have shown music can slow heart rates and reduce blood pressure. Some hospitals now play music in delivery rooms to calm mothers giving birth and in obstetric rooms, because babies born with physical problems respond better to treatment when music is played. Other studies have shown music can improve post-operative pain and anxiety. Songs such as Pachabel's *Canon in D* have a calming effect on those in the recovery room.

In a study at The Chelsea and Westminster Hospital in London, patients who listened to live music needed less medication and recovered more quickly than those who did not listen to music at all.[11]

At the Body-Mind Wellness Center in Meadville, Pennsylvania, Dr. Barry Bittman and his co-workers put 32 volunteers in stressful situations. They then took blood samples to measure the effect on stress-related genes. The results showed the genes firing like crazy during the episodes of stress (trying to solve an almost impossible jigsaw puzzle in a short time). Then a portion of the volunteers participated in a music playing session. After having a little fun playing music, blood tests showed nearly half (19 out of 45) of the markers for the stress genes had reversed, while those who just sat and read magazines reversed only six of these markers.[12]

I could go on and on as the research on music and medicine continues every day. There are also a number of very good books on this subject.

Dr. Mitchell Gaynor believes music is so powerful that it can help cure cancer. In his book, *The Healing Power of Sound: Recovery from Life-Threatening Illness Using Sound, Voice, and Music*, Gaynor cites case after case where he has used music – specifically Tibetan Singing

Bowls – to improve the condition of patients. Some physicians believe his techniques could revolutionize medicine and healing.

There is some fascinating information in his book, and it is well worth the day or two you will need to read it. Gaynor has also authored *Sounds of Healing: A Physician Reveals the Therapeutic Power of Sound, Voice, and Music.*

Richard Katz, a former Harvard Professor who wrote *Boiling Energy: Community Healing among the Kalahari Kung,* reports to have seen wounds close and heal through the power of music. Katz has studied the Kalahari Kung tribe of central Africa where he has witnessed singing and dancing circles aimed at healing injury and terminal illnesses. In one incident, a man's wounds from a lion attack closed over, stopped bleeding, and were barely visible after 20 healers sang, drummed, chanted, and danced around him through the night.

In *The Tao of Music: Sound Psychology,* author John M. Ortiz, Ph. D., outlines how he uses music in his psychology practice to help patients overcome depression. One of the techniques Ortiz outlines is having patients create their own mix tapes or CDs with selections designed to take them from sad to happy. For example, three songs that match the current mood (sad, depressed, etc.), three songs with a better tempo to move in a positive direction, and then songs that make them happy. The book contains 41 exercises that use music to improve your life – from reducing stress to enhancing creativity.

I say one good thing, one good thing
When it hits you feel no pain
One good thing about music
When it hits you feel no pain
So hit me with music
Hit me with music now
  – Bob Marley, Trenchtown Rock

P L A Y   M E   A   M E L O D Y

In Australia, the Didgeridoo, a musical instrument used by the Aborigines, is now being used to treat sleep disorders. A report in the *British Medical Journal* indicated that people with sleep apnea who took four months of didgeridoo lessons had less daytime sleepiness and snored significantly less.[13] Playing the instrument exercises and strengthens tissues in the mouth and throat which helps prevent the tongue from obstructing the airway.

One explanation for music's amazing powers comes from author and musician, Joshua Leeds. In his book, *The Power of Sound*, Leeds points to the relationship of the ear to a specific cranial nerve. The nerve, called the vagus, wanders through the abdominal and thoracic cavities. In doing so, it helps regulate the functions of various organs – including the heart, lungs, stomach, and liver.

Leeds concludes that this interconnectivity allows music to enter through the ear and communicate directly to these organs. For this reason, Leeds believes sound, and what we choose to hear, has a direct effect on our health. *"The ear brings in energy that touches us from the top to bottom. Sound is not just vibrating the eardrum. It is actually resonating the entire being,"* Leeds writes in the book.

He also reports on the work of French sound researcher Fabien Maman, who has documented the destruction of cancer cells with the music from a xylophone.

The Power of Sound has a wealth of information on sound and music research, as well as a CD with music Leeds composed to improve your health. The songs are classical selections he says he has enhanced for a fuller effect.

THE BEAT GOES ON

Both Leeds and Dr. Gaynor write about the phenomenon of entrainment – where two vibrating bodies try to synchronize with each other. The best example of this is tuning forks where one fork will cause another fork of the same frequency to vibrate.

The phenomenon is not limited to music. People find the sound of the ocean relaxing because they end up synchronizing their breathing with the crashing of the waves. There are even examples of female college roommates having synchronized menstrual cycles after living together for several months. My sisters (I have six of them) tell me this happened while growing up in our home as well.

When reading Leed's book, I was in my favorite recliner slowly rocking back and forth. I started thinking about entrainment and, sure enough, when I checked – my rocking matched the rhythm of my heartbeat. I rocked forward on one beat, rocked back on the next.

Leeds and Gaynor both mention the work of the late Dr. Alfred Tomatis, an expert in the field of therapeutic music and sound. A French ENT (ear, nose, and throat physician), Tomatis did groundbreaking work on how people listen.

Tomatis was able to determine that singers could not sing tones they were unable to hear. He also found that opera singers suffered hearing loss from singing too loudly. (Tomatis' father was a famous opera singer and inspired his work.) Through experimentation, Tomatis developed something called the "Electronic Ear." This device is used to strengthen muscles in the middle ear to restore hearing loss. He also focused on improving the way people listen. Through this research, he believed he could improve a singer's voice range. He used the same techniques to improve learning skills and even a person's energy.

The Tomatis Method is now also used to help patients with attention deficit disorders, learning delays, balance and coordination problems, Asperger's Syndrome, and even autism. You can learn more about the Tomatis Center's work at www.tomatis.com. There are a number of Tomatis treatment centers now located in the United States and Canada.

Another unique method of treatment is called Brain Music Therapy. In this therapy, the music comes from the patient's own mind. Developed at the Moscow Medical Academy in 1991, the technique starts by doing an electroencephalogram, or EEG, on the patient. The unique brain waves are then converted to musical notes and transferred to a compact disc.

There are two tracks of music on the CD, one for relaxation and the other to energize. Brain Music Therapy has been used to reduce stress, insomnia, anxiety, and depression and has been found to increase productivity and concentration. It can be helpful to anyone, and it has been used in treating bipolar disorders and autism.

I do not believe, however, that if you get a song stuck in your head (the earworm effect) that it will end up on the CD. You can learn more about this treatment at www. BrainMusicTreatment.com.

By the way, in that movie, *The Music Man*, even though the con man, Professor Harold Hill, has no idea how to teach music, the boys in the town learn to play a song just by thinking about it. There may have been some truth in that fictional story after all.

THE ZEN TEN

Songs to get stuck in your head

1. Dream On – Aerosmith
2. All You Need Is Love – The Beatles
3. Get Up Stand Up – Bob Marley
4. Part Of The Plan – Dan Fogelberg
5. Change The World – Eric Clapton

6. You've Got A Friend – James Taylor
7. Instant Karma! – John Lennon
8. Your Life Is Now – John Mellencamp
9. I Saw The Sign – Ace of Base
10. Stand – Rascal Flatts

* For more great "earworm" songs, visit www.BetterSoundAdvice. com

SOUND SUGGESTIONS

Remember These Tips From This Chapter

1. Use music or rhythm to help with learning and memorization.
2. Investigate Music Therapy to help in treatment of illness.
3. Learn to play music, any instrument, to help keep your brain active and reduce stress.
4. End each drive or break with positive music to get a good earworm stuck in your head.

Notes

There's a guy in my block, he lives for rock
He plays records day and night
And when he feels down, he puts some rock n roll on
And it makes him feel alright
  *– **The Kinks, A Rock and Roll Fantasy***

MOOD MUSIC

What is your mood like on a daily basis? Are you aware of how your mood changes depending on the environment and situation? Will a better mood improve success in these situations? After all, everyone else is trying to control your mood. Why not do it yourself?

When was the last time you were in an elevator and heard anything other than easy listening, instrumental songs? No Heavy Metal to get you riled up in an enclosed environment with a bunch of people you may or may not know. Those who own the elevators want you to remain calm during your ride up or down.

At the supermarket, and many other retail locations, the sounds you hear are intended to entice you to spend more money. Studies have shown that when slow music is played in the grocery store, shoppers stay longer and spend more money (39 percent more) than if fast music is played.[14]

At a fast food or chain restaurant, you are more likely to hear upbeat music. Studies show it speeds up customers so they will spend less time taking up space at their tables. Fast music and fast meals means more customers. In addition, do not be surprised if the establishment is playing French music when it is pushing its French wine or tropical music with tropical drinks. The combination has proven to boost sales.

Ronald Milliman, a marketing professor at Western Kentucky University, conducted a study at an upscale Texas restaurant and found patrons stayed an average of 11 minutes longer with slow music compared to fast music, and the bar bills were nearly 50 percent higher.[15]

An experiment in the faculty and staff cafeteria at Fairfield University showed that people took an average of over one bite of food more per minute when fast music was played compared to no music at all. On the other end of the scale, in the Hard Rock Café in Orlando, the music gets slower the closer it gets to closing time – which naturally causes the customers to begin to leave.

What causes this reaction? Neurological studies show rhythmic drumming at certain frequencies can make the brain's rhythms become synchronized to them. Research at the Spring Creek Institute in Durham, North Carolina, suggests certain types of drumming produces these powerful effects by driving the electrical rhythms in the brain.[16]

THE STARBUCKS SOUND

At Starbucks, much of their business philosophy is focused on making you comfortable in their stores. From the furniture to the music and, of course, the coffee, the goal is to make Starbucks the "third place" in your life behind home and the office. The music, referred to as the "Starbucks Sound," is aimed at drawing you into the store and keeping you there. This sound has become so popular, Starbucks now co-produces its own CDs and even has a channel on XM Radio, Starbucks XM Café (Channel 45.)

While you may hear the occasional Ray Charles, Bob Dylan, or Ella Fitzgerald tune, most of the songs are probably new to you. The typical reaction is, "I don't know that song, but I like it." Often jazzy and never too loud, Starbucks aim is not to disrupt that cup of coffee or Grande, low-fat, mocha latte that you are enjoying. Odds are that when you walk out you will be toting one of their CDs in your hand. Music sales have become a significant source of revenue for the Seattle-based company.

Not long ago, I had a business meeting at a Starbucks in Chicago. We chose some comfortable chairs near the front of the store to talk but were not able to get much done at first. The music was much louder than normal and not the usual "sound" you hear there. I found myself annoyed not so much because I was having a hard time hearing the others at the meeting, but because the experience was not what I had become accustomed to when visiting Starbucks. I expected a certain mood for this meeting and did not get it. After a brief discussion with an employee, the music changed and so did my mood.

MMRS is an acronym for Music Mood Regulatory Scale. This is a real way to assess the effectiveness of music as a mood-regulating strategy. Findings from studies on MMRS show that the more a person believes certain behaviors or processes will improve their mood, the more likely that listening to music will help alleviate anger, depression, and tension. When I heard the wrong music at Starbucks, my mood scale definitely did not improve. On the other hand, I believe that up-tempo music will help me exercise and, as a result, it always does.

A 1999 study by marketing professor James Kellaris (the earworm guy) at the University of Cincinnati found the music you listen to while on hold affects both your mood and the perception of time. While most people thought they were on hold longer than they actually were, some types of music made the wait seem shorter. This is important since an Associated Press (AP) poll in May 2006 found more than half of Americans (54 percent) lose their patience if kept on hold more than five minutes.[17]

Classical music had a more calming effect on men in Kellaris' study, while women preferred light jazz. Rock music had more of an aggravating effect on most callers. In the AP study, a majority preferred music to talk radio or company ads while on hold.

Pump Up the Volume

The *Journal of Sports Sciences* reported in 2005 that listening to music prior to competition increases the positive mood states of individuals participating in sports and exercise. The results produced moods often associated with optimal performance.

Why not use the same strategy for your everyday life?

At the Institute for Music, Health and Education, founder Don Campbell says music can cause measurable changes in body function. It can relax, energize, change skin temperature, and improve cardiovascular function . . . all of which can improve your mood.

Campbell is not alone in these beliefs. Dr. Sherman Vander Ark, professor of music at the University of Akron, discovered that listening to classical music could change the neural chemistry of the blood.[18] The effect is an enhanced feeling of well-being and an enriched ability to learn.

The most stunning information from Vander Ark's research is that music helped to balance the levels of cortisol (a hormone that helps the body manage stress) and increased the levels of norepinephrine and endorphins (neurotransmitters that have pain-relieving properties similar to morphine) by as much as 30 percent.

A study at Michigan State University in 1993 had similar results. Participants who listened to their preferred choice of music lowered levels of cortisol by as much as 25 percent and increased by more than 10 percent the levels of interleukin-1 (an immune-cell messenger molecule that helps to regulate the activity of other immune cells).[19]

While music is effective in changing your mood, I am not suggesting you wear the headphones 24/7 and shut out the rest of the world. There are key times each day, however, when a little music can lift your spirits.

TUNE IN, TURN ON

Did you wake up on the wrong side of bed? Have you discovered that you do not want to deal with people until after that first cup of coffee? The secret to getting your day off to a good start could lie in what you hear, not what you drink.

Playing music you really enjoy – in the shower, while getting dressed, or while driving to work – can set the tone of your day right from the start. You can use the "earworm" effect to your advantage – get a song you like stuck in your head. The choice of music type really does not seem to matter, as long as it has a positive effect on your mood.

Students at Penn State University, Altoona, were told to listen to music they enjoyed and to record their feelings over a two-week period. Rock, easy listening, classical, oldies, it did not matter what style; the music helped the students feel more optimistic, relaxed, and friendly.

Researchers Valerie N. Stratton, PhD, a psychology teacher, and Annette H. Zalanowski, a music teacher, both of PSU-Altoona, reported their findings in a *Psychology and Education: an Interdisciplinary Journal (2003)*. "Not only did our sample of students report more positive emotions after listening to music, but their already positive emotions were intensified by listening to music," Stratton was quoted as saying in a news release from Penn State University. Therefore, if you happen to be in a good mood already when you wake up, music can make it even better. You can then turn these good feelings into good ideas.

New research in 2008 found that when you are in a positive mood, you are more likely to choose creative activities.[20] The study released through the Indiana University Department of Psychological and Brain Sciences showed a strong link between positive mood and creativity. "One thing we discovered in our research is that people are aware of the fact that being creative makes them feel good, and so tasks that afford potential for creativity are particularly appealing when in a positive mood," said Edward Hirt, associate professor in the Department of Psychological and Brain Sciences at IU Bloomington.

C U B I C L E   C O N C E R T

When there's too much to do
Don't let it bother you, forget your troubles,
Try to be just like a cheerful chick-a-dee
And whistle while you work
Come on get smart, tune up and start
To whistle while you work
    *– **Snow White and the Seven Dwarfs***

The Seven Dwarfs may have been on to something when they told everyone to "whistle while you work" way back in 1937. The song from the Disney children's classic encourages a good mood even while doing the most menial of tasks – and apparently, that works.

A study done by the University of Illinois found that employees who listen to music at work do perform better. The results reported in the *Journal of Applied Psychology (October, 1995)* indicated that employees randomly selected to bring their stereos into work with them exhibited significant improvement in mood, job performance, and satisfaction with their organization. The employees wore headsets to listen (so they did not disturb others) and those with the relatively simple jobs responded most positively. The results were less positive on those who were on the phone a lot or had work that is more complex.

Surgeons often will play classical music in the operating room to help them relax and concentrate. Teachers play baroque and other classical music in the classroom to help achieve that "Mozart effect" thought to be conducive to learning. Moreover, those working in sales have been known to play an inspiring tune or two just prior to meeting with a potential client. If you can get away with having music play lightly in the background at work, do it. It can help set your mood and allow you to perform your best.

A few years back, the folks in the Long Term Care division of General Electric (now Genworth Financial) asked their sales managers for the name of the song they like to play before going on a sales call. They compiled the list of tunes and put them on a CD that was distributed to the entire sales force. The first song on the CD? *Start Me Up* by The Rolling Stones.

Among the many playlists I have compiled on my iPod is one named Work Background. These songs are mostly instrumental and classical. The idea is to have something that stimulates but also allows me to concentrate on the task at hand. (I listened to this playlist as I wrote most of this book.)

This strategy even works for cows and chickens. Psychologists at the University of Leicester in the United Kingdom were able to increase milk production in cattle by three percent when relaxing music was played in the milking shed. *Moon River, Bridge over Troubled Water,* and *Everybody Hurts* were all big hits with Bessie and company.[21]

The research was done on the heels of anecdotal evidence that showed playing music for chickens helped reduce stress in the birds and improved egg production. There is no report on whether playing *The Chicken Dance* produced more eggs or is reserved for chicken aerobic classes.

I suggest you also compile a playlist, CDs, or tapes that you can play throughout your workday depending on the situation – something inspirational before a big client meeting, something to relax to after a stressful event, and something to play in the background at work that helps keep you plugging along. After all, many classical songs were composed as background music for dinners and other social events held by royalty and aristocrats of that time.

A Song in Your Heart

Hearing music is proven to have very positive effects on your mood throughout the day. You can gain even more benefits by singing or playing music at least once a day. One of my more recent fond memories involved a family trip to visit friends at Lake of the Ozarks. After dinner one evening, our hosts, Luke and Shannon, took us for a cruise down the extensive waterway and played some of our favorite classic rock songs. Everyone joined in, singing along at the top of their lungs. It took a while for the smiles to leave our faces and for the good feelings to subside.

There is a general feeling among humans that if someone is singing, everything must be okay. Some tribes in Africa even believe singing can help cure illnesses. In almost every religion, many prayers are sung rather than spoken. The belief is that singing the sacred words intensify the communication with the one to whom you are praying.

The effect singing has on your body is two-fold. First, the act of singing is an emotional expression. This, by itself, can be very stimulating. Add the fact you are bringing in more oxygen to your system, and you can feel the increase in energy throughout your body. Singing can be a mild form of exercise, because it increases heart rate and the flow of oxygen. As a result, singing has been linked to lower blood pressure, lower heart rate, and lower stress. It has also been shown to help alleviate pain.

Every day when I get home from work
I feel so frustrated
The boss is a jerk
And I get my sticks and go out to the shed
And I pound on that drum like it was the boss's head
Because
I don't want to work
I want to bang on the drum all day
   *– **Todd Rundgren, Bang the Drum All Day***

P L A Y   I T   A G A I N ,   J O E Y

Playing music can have similar effects. It takes movement to play and, in some cases, can be physically exhausting. Even better, it can be an excellent way to relieve stress. A recent study of workers in a high burnout industry found that when they participated in drum-beating sessions, they experienced a 50 percent improvement in mood that lasted for weeks.[22] At St. Mary's Cancer Center in Evansville, Indiana, patients participate in "drum circles" to promote healing, relaxation, and group harmony.

For Joey Coogan of Des Plaines, Illinois, pounding the drums certainly made a difference in his life – it helped him beat leukemia. After being diagnosed with the deadly disease at age 10, the Children's Wish Network granted Joey his wish: a brand new drum set. He played the drums at home, at early morning school band sessions, and in the evenings with the school jazz band. By age 13, Joey was cured, and he told me his leukemia is completely gone.

"I don't know if it (playing the drums) helped with the cancer directly, but it helped me with my mental health," Joey said. "My chemotherapy was really intense for a while and playing made me feel a lot better. I guess one of the mysteries of music is why it makes us feel the way it does. I don't know if it made a difference with my leukemia, but I was happier when I played."

Joey's mother, Anne Coogan, was devastated when she learned of Joey's diagnosis. She says she was upset and somewhat lost. Anne had heard about therapists using music to treat mental health but did not realize it was also used in the treatment of cancer. She says Joey's music therapist at Yakman Children's Pavillion/Lutheran General hospital in Parkridge, Illinois, invited him to join a drumming group with other teenagers. Anne then witnessed the difference it made in Joey.

"He became more relaxed when he played, and it put Joey in a much better mood," Anne told me. "I thought it made a difference because I think everything that helped him maintain a positive attitude throughout the whole experience was very valuable to his therapy."

THE THRILL OF VICTORY

Believe it or not, music can provide more thrills than sex (bear with me on this one). Avram Goldstein, a pharmacologist at Stanford University, found brain chemicals may be involved in one's intense enjoyment of music. Goldstein studies what gives people "thrills," special feelings brought on by sudden changes in emotion. Respondents in his study mentioned thrills occurring in response to music (96 percent) more often than thrills in response to sexual activity (70 percent).[23] Goldstein also found that people had a similar thrill each time they listened to a certain piece of music, although the intensity varied.

The experience can be even greater when the music is tied to a particular event or experience. Who doesn't get a few chills or goose bumps each time they hear the screeching violins in *Psycho's* shower scene or the pulsating cello in *Jaws* as the shark is about to attack? Who hasn't done a little shadow boxing when the theme from *Rocky, Eye of the Tiger*, is playing? I cannot help but smile when I hear that cheesy ballad, *Superstar* by The Carpenters, because it makes me think of the car scene from *Tommy Boy* – one of my all-time favorite comedies.

The folks in Hollywood are masters at creating a mood with music in its movies. Soundtracks can make or break a movie. A soundtrack for your life can help get you through your day in a much better mood.

The time's real short, you know the distance is long
I'd rather have a jet but it's not in the song
Climb back in the cab, cross your fingers for luck
We gotta keep movin' if we're going to make a buck.
Let it roll down the highway
  – Bachman Turner Overdrive, Roll On Down The Highway

D R I V I N G   B E A T

As a member of the Baby Boom generation, I spent a lot of time and money on sound systems for my cars when I was younger. Nowhere near what some kids are spending today but, it was important for me to have some good tunes to play on my car cassette for that big date. (I am proud to say I never owned an 8-track player but knew plenty of friends who did.)

Of course, despite my hopes and dreams, I spent a lot more time listening to those tunes by myself or with friends instead of on dates. To this day, listening to music while I am driving is important to me. My CD player, XM Radio, and iPod all get regular use. The choice of music, however, is a little different than my teenage years.

Dealing with rush hour traffic, the clogged toll ways surrounding Chicago, or any other major city used to frustrate me to no end. That is until I decided to change my tune(s). Now I have a playlist and CDs labeled "Relax." The song selection is filled with music from John Coltrane, Charlie Parker, and various classical composers. The music does relax me, and I do not seem to mind how long it takes to get to my next destination.

Since many people still drive to and from work, this is a good time to play music that will help improve your mood. Your attitude heading into work or on the way home to be with your family can make a big difference in how happy you, and consequently, those around you are. It can also make the drive much safer.

Virgin Cars of the United Kingdom polled their customers and found Heavy Metal was the most popular music to listen to while driving, despite the fact that it can be the most distracting.[24] Play this kind of music at a high volume and you are twice as likely to run a red light. Research from Israel also found people listening to up-tempo music while driving had double the number of accidents of those listening to slower music.[25]

A preference for Heavy Metal music has been tied to participation in reckless or dangerous activities. So much so it has been banned (along with Rap) from some classrooms in London. Behind the wheel of a car is probably not the best place to be listening to it at high volumes. Instead, choose less distracting types of music played at lower volumes to help keep you alert and relaxed.

THE ZEN TEN

Songs to help put you in a better mood

1. Good Vibrations – The Beach Boys
2. Here Comes The Sun – The Beatles
3. How Sweet It Is – Marvin Gaye
4. Revival – The Allman Brothers Band
5. I'm Alright – Kenny Loggins
6. Always Look On The Bright Side Of Life – Monty Python
7. Crazy Little Thing Called Love – Queen
8. Hold On To Your Dream – Stevie Wonder
9. You Can Call Me Al – Paul Simon
10. Bright Side Of The Road – Van Morrison

* For more great mood-enhancing songs, visit www. BetterSoundAdvice.com

SOUND SUGGESTIONS

Remember These Tips From This Chapter

1. Start your morning off with music to get you in a good mood.
2. Be aware of music in your surroundings and how it affects your mood.
3. Listen to light background music at work.
4. Listen to up tempo music to prepare for competition or a big meeting.
5. Sing or play music when you can – at church, school, parties, in the shower, etc.
6. Choose the proper playlist for your drive time.
7. Turn off the cell phone the last 10 minutes of your drive home to separate work and family. Bring a good mood home with you.

Notes

So much to do so much to see
So what's wrong with taking the back streets
You'll never know if you don't go
You'll never shine if you don't glow
Hey now you're an All Star get your game on, go
play
    *– **Smash Mouth, All Star***

CHAPTER FOUR – SOUND MACHINE
FIT AS A FIDDLE

Do you remember the movie *Billie*? Probably not. The film from 1965 did not win any awards. Both the plot and acting were pretty weak. I did not see the film until Billie made its way to the television screen a few years later.

Two things made this movie memorable for me. First was the appearance of a young Patty Duke (better known now as the mother of *Rudy* star Sean Astin). The second was the storyline – a young girl who could run faster than the boys because she heard "the beat" in her head. "The beat, you see, I hear it up here (*pointing to her brain*) and when I want to go faster I speed up the beat and I go," Duke's character, Billie, says in the movie. The music she heard was not all that great – it was from Hollywood in the 60s. However, the thought of music helping you run faster intrigued me. Was this fact or Hollywood fiction?

Before the days of the iPod, I tried running while wearing bulky headphones without much luck. Now, running is too hard on my knees, so I mostly walk at a brisk pace or use an elliptical trainer. However, the ear buds and iPod I wear have a positive effect on both my pace and my mood. The beat in the songs gets me going.

Study after study has shown that adding music to your exercise routine results in a better workout. Remember *Sweatin' To The Oldies*? Richard Simmons sold millions of copies of the exercise videos. The exercise routines amounted to little more than standing in front of your television and doing some light cardio movements to the rock music of the 50s and 60s. I am not sure how many of those videos still get regular use, but thanks to the mp3 player, you can now take the oldies, or any other high tempo music, with you while you exercise. Not only does music inspire movement, it also helps the time go by faster. For distance runners, the music allows them to focus on something other than the miles and fatigue. For the average person, it provides a rhythm for movement.

No way, you can fight it every day
But no matter what you say
You know it
The rhythm is gonna get'cha
No clue, of what's happening to you
And before this night is through
Ooh baby
The rhythm is gonna get'cha
  *– **Gloria Estefan, Rhythm is Gonna Get You***

TUNE UP

In 2002, researchers at the United States Sports Academy in Alabama reported that running with music, "...clearly demonstrates that the playing of music had a profound effect on participants in the study."[26]

In the study, the average lap time of the runners listening to music decreased by three seconds per lap in trained subjects and five seconds per lap in untrained subjects – an improvement of nearly 10 percent for the untrained runners.

The most interesting results from the study were that while the music-listening participants ran faster, their heart rates actually decreased compared to non-music-listening runners' heart rates. The music seemed to make their hearts beat more efficiently, perhaps a result of a better rhythm in their strides or because of entrainment, the phenomenon where rhythms in nature tend to synchronize.

Running is not the only exercise affected by music. Research done at the University of Wisconsin—La Crosse in 2003 showed that people listening to up-tempo music got a lot more out of their stationary bike workouts. Music caused them to pedal faster – between 5 percent and 15 percent harder – and produce more power output than with no music.[27] Their heart rates increased with the tempo of the music: 133 beats per minute (bpm) on average for no music; 140 bpm for slow music; and 146 bpm for medium and fast music.

What music will work best for you depends on your personal preferences. Research at Brunel University in England found that listening to the songs you like before and during exercise will not only reduce feelings of tiredness, it will also increase performance levels by up to 20 per cent.[28]

Researcher Dr. Costas Karageorghis of Brunel's School of Sport and Education suggests people select songs that drive them and inspire them, then align the songs with their workout to get maximum performance. For more information on the study, and a chart indicating the different music styles used to reach target heart rates, visit Brunel's Web site at: http://www.brunel.ac.uk/ news/pressoffice/pressreleases/2005/cdata/october/ Costas+music.

In addition, the *Journal of Medicine & Science in Sports & Exercise* found that people who exercised while listening to their favorite songs worked out longer and at a higher intensity.[29]

Alison Hoye, a certified fitness instructor with the National Institute for Fitness and Sport, sees the effect music has on workouts every day. She incorporates music into her classes and training sessions.

"If you are at the peak of a workout, a song that revs you up can help you get through that last intense interval," Hoye told me. "Likewise, a calming song is perfect for a cool down. Music helps in establishing a cadence, so the beats per minute serve a functional purpose by encouraging the exerciser to maintain whatever pace the song dictates. This can't be done in silence."

The use of music while exercising has also spread to a sport known for being somewhat quiet and reserved – tennis. An exercise class called Cardio Tennis has become popular at tennis facilities across the nation. The workout features constant movement and drills on the court combined with high-energy music in the background. You can learn more about Cardio Tennis and where you can participate at www.cardiotennis.com. I have done Cardio Tennis a few times, and it was a great workout and helped my tennis game as well.

At the local YMCA, I am not alone in hitting the elliptical machine or treadmill armed with an mp3 player. The others I see listening to music seem to be enjoying themselves more while exercising and appear to be more focused than those without headphones.

Several years ago, instead of music, I listened to the audio from the television sets mounted in the cardio room at the Y. It helped me stay current with the news of the day (thanks to *Morning Express* with Robin Meade on CNN Headline News) but the workouts were not nearly as intense as they are now that I have switched to music. (Sorry, Robin. I still watch, but with closed captions.)

It turns out watching television may actually have a negative effect on exercise results. A 1996 study of a group of women found they worked 5 percent harder when exercising with the TV off compared to with it on.[30]

Now before you begin an exercise program, with or without music, you should consult your doctor to rule out any potential health risks. Your physician can also help you determine what type and level of exercise is best suited for you. If you are already exercising on a regular basis, great. If not, get started as soon as you can.

Walk this Way

America is fat and getting fatter. Statistics compiled in 2006 by Trust for America's Health (www. healthamericans.org), a group that promotes increased funding for health programs, show that nearly two-thirds of adult Americans are overweight, and 1-out-of-4 is considered medically obese. Even more concerning, 1-out-of-6 children are overweight.

All these extra pounds lead to increased health problems – including diabetes and hypertension – and significant increases in the cost of health care.[31] To make matters worse, being fat can also make you dumber and increase your risk of Alzheimer's disease.

Swedish researchers found that higher Body Mass Indexes (BMIs) are more likely to lead to a loss of brain tissue.[32] The brain atrophy was found in the temporal lobe, which controls, among other things, memory, comprehension, and visual processing. How the increased weight affects the brain is not yet known, but researchers speculate one reason could be that fat causes the release of hormones that are harmful to brain tissue, which leads to brain atrophy and an increased risk of Alzheimer's disease.

America's obesity problem is caused by two main factors: poor eating habits and a lack of regular exercise. A 2004 CDC (Centers for Disease Control and Prevention) report indicated that if just ten percent of Americans began a regular walking program, it would save the country over five billion dollars in heart disease costs.

Walking is an excellent form of exercise. It does not take a toll on your body and joints the way running may. If the music alone does not motivate you to get up and move, schedule regular walks with your spouse or a friend. When you schedule an exercise session with someone else, you are much more likely to keep that appointment and keep yourself accountable.

Add music to your walking routine and you will have a better chance of losing weight. At Fairleigh Dickinson University's School of Psychology, director Christopher Capuano and his research team put this theory to the test in 2005.[33]

Capuano's team put 41 overweight to moderately obese women through a program of dieting, walking, and group meetings designed to promote healthier lifestyles. All were expected to walk two miles, three times per week. Half were told to listen to music of their choice while walking, the other half walked without music.

After six months, the music group followed the program nearly exactly as instructed (98 percent) and lost twice as much weight (16 pounds versus 8 pounds for the non-music group). Only 68 percent of the non-music group adhered to the program. The loss of body fat of the music group also doubled, four percent versus two percent.

After reading about this study in an article on the Internet, a woman wrote to Capuano and backed up his findings. "I feel compelled to tell you that without my CD player, I would not have lost 30 pounds (and counting)," she wrote. "Music is essential to my workout. I make mixed music CDs and arrange the upbeat songs to create a 30-minute workout including a warm-up song, some "work hard" songs, and then a cool-down song. Thought you might recommend this technique because it really works!"

To be successful with any exercise program, even walking, you need to WANT to do it. I do not know how many times I have heard someone say, "I really need to start exercising." The problem is that often this "need" is not enough motivation to get started.

FEEL THE NEED

You probably know people who have been ordered by their doctor to start exercising and to lose weight and still do not do it. This is something you have to REALLY want to do. Unfortunately, some people see exercise as boring and cannot seem to find the motivation to get moving. That is where music can help. It may be that one little thing that makes the difference between a *couch potato* and a *road warrior*.

It helps if the company you work for offers incentives for improving your health – such as gym memberships or reduced health insurance premiums. Some health insurance companies also are finding ways to improve the health of their members through things like Health Incentive Accounts (HIAs) or rewards programs – such as WellPoint's *Healthy Lifestyles* (www.FindAHealthierYou.com) – where members can earn free sports gear, electronic equipment or clothing if they follow a recommended exercise program.

There are also the options of aerobic classes at your local gym. More and more of these classes include music to help with motivation. Step Aerobics, Cardio Cycling, Power Pump, and Mega Jam are all examples of classes at my local YMCA that include music.

Not long ago it added Drums Alive, a dancing and drumming class that, according to the YMCA Web site, ". . . releases endorphins and releases negative feelings. The rhythmical patterns of the drum increases synchronization of brain wave activity, which in turn provides feelings of euphoria and improved mental awareness and self-acceptance. This is a unique, fun, exciting alternative to traditional aerobics."

The most important thing is to find a way to make exercise fun. If it is fun, you are more likely to want to exercise on a regular basis. If the motivation is there, the results and benefits of exercise will likely follow. Research has shown that as little as 30 minutes of exercise on a regular basis can alleviate depression, enhance your mood, and improve your well-being long term. More intense exercise boosts endorphins to greater levels. Research on runners showed people who went on a two-hour run filled the emotion and mood-controlling regions of their brain with the feel-good hormones – the runner's high you hear so much about.

THE ZEN TEN

Songs to help you get more from exercise

1. Let's Get It Started – Black Eyed Peas
2. Superstition – Stevie Wonder
3. Start Me Up – The Rolling Stones
4. Working My Way Back To You – The Spinners

5. Shining Star – Earth, Wind & Fire
6. Ramblin' Man – The Allman Brothers
7. I Don't Wanna Go On With You Like That – Elton John
8. Take It Easy – The Eagles
9. Life is a Highway – Rascal Flatts
10. The South's Gonna Do It Again – Charlie Daniels Band

* For more great workout songs, visit www.BetterSoundAdvice.com

SOUND SUGGESTIONS

Remember These Tips From This Chapter

1. Use music when you workout. Have a variety of tunes to keep you motivated.
2. Consult a physician before beginning any exercise program.
3. Sign up for an exercise program that uses music to motivate.

Notes

MY EXERCISE PLAYLIST

For 45 minutes of exercise including warm-up and cool-down

1. I'll Play The Blues For You – Bryan Lee – Bryan Lee's Greatest Hits
2. Jingo – Santana – Live at the Fillmore 1968
3. Mary Had A Little Lamb – Stevie Ray Vaughan – Live Alive
4. Sing, Sing, Sing – The Benny Goodman Orchestra – Benny Goodman Selected Favorites, Volume 5
5. Rock and a Hard Place – The Rolling Stones – Steel Wheels
6. Soul Sacrifice – Santana – The Best of Santana
7. I'm Not Running Anymore – John Mellencamp – Words and Music
8. Stand – Rascal Flatts – Me and My Gang

MORE GREAT WORKOUT SONGS

From Alison Hoye, WellPoint Wellness Center Manager, National Institute for Fitness and Sport

1. Tear Me Down – Hedwig and the Angry Inch
2. Fergalicious – Fergie
3. Nothin' but a Good Time – Poison
4. Free Me – Emma Bunton
5. Mama Said Knock You Out – L.L. Cool J
6. Everything is Beautiful – Static Revenger
7. American Woman – Lenny Kravitz
8. Do It To It – Cherish
9. Crank That (edited version) – Soulja Boy
10. Toxic – Britney Spears
11. Ray of Light – Madonna
12. Vertigo – U2
13. All Things (Just Keep Getting Better) – Wildlife
14. Where the Party At – Jagged Edge
15. Beverly Hills – Weezer

16. Heaven Must be Missing an Angel – Tavares
17. Soldier – Destiny's Child
18. You Make Me Feel (Mighty Real) - Sylvester
19. Chains of Love – Erasure
20. The Jump Off (edited version) – Lil' Kim

Go-Go music really makes us dance
Do the pony puts us in a trance
Do the watusi just give us a chance
That's then we fall in line
We got the beat
Yeah
We got the beat
   *– **The Go Go's, We Got The Beat***

DANCE THE POUNDS AWAY

My father is one heck of a dancer. At age 85, he is still so light on his feet that all the guys watch in amazement while the women stand in line hoping for a chance to have him lead them around the dance floor.

He grew up in the era of the Big Bands. The music they played was meant to get people on the dance floor – and by people, I mean couples. Rarely, in those days, did anyone dance alone. You grabbed your partner by the hand and moved together in rhythm to the music.

Dad met my mother when both were teaching dance lessons at Arthur Murray studios. They were a hit on the dance floor and an even bigger hit together in life.

Since my mother died when I was young (age 7), I do not have many memories of them dancing. I can imagine how wonderful they were together, however, when I see him dance with my younger sister, Jackie. Early on, Dad taught her all his favorite dances. As Jackie blossomed into a young woman, she would go with Dad to all the local performances of Big Band groups. They put on dancing exhibitions that left everyone in awe.

This exercise from all the dancing over the years kept him slim and trim . . . and probably saved Dad's life. At age 79 he told his doctor he felt a little flutter in his upper chest area when he danced. Further examination found significant blockage in arteries around his heart.

A quintuple bypass was needed to prevent an inevitable heart attack.

The surgery knocked him off the dance floor for several months. His recovery went better, however, than most who have gone through that at his age. Dad felt it was because the dancing kept him in shape. Not long after the bypass, he was back cutting a rug.

In the summer of 2005, at age 82, Dad impressed everyone again at my niece's wedding reception. Even the DJ asked him to stay out on the floor to show the youngsters how to dance. Dad can only go a few songs now before he needs to rest, but a wonderful moment came for me when he danced with my daughter, Katie. She enjoyed that dance with her grandpa so much that she wanted to learn more. She took up swing dancing that fall during her freshman year in college.

It turns out dancing has some significant aerobic benefits. Many swing dancing participants have been known to get their pulse up to 60 percent of their maximum heart rate – as much as a low-impact cardio workout at the gym. Men and women can burn between 400 and 800 calories per hour swing dancing. This is one of the reasons for the resurgence of swing dancing clubs across the country. Not only can you get in a good workout, the social interaction is an important added benefit. Research indicates this is very important to both adults and children.

Former NFL star wide receiver Jerry Rice is among those who have become a fan of dancing for exercise. His participation on ABC's *Dancing with the Stars* produced some surprising results. "I lost 14 pounds during those eight weeks of dancing—and, at 212 pounds, I was in good shape to begin with," Rice was quoted as saying in

Parade Magazine (July 2, 2006). "But I liked the way my body changed. I stayed strong yet became leaner, more flexible and fluid."

That same article pointed out that the benefits of dancing are more than physical. A study of 500 seniors found regular dancing lowered the risk of mental decline as we age. The researchers believe dancing increases blood flow to the brain, improves thought processes by learning new routines, and keeps older folks from feeling alone.

The popularity of dancing has increased significantly thanks to shows such as *Dancing with the Stars, So You Think You Can Dance,* and others. Video games have also played a role in getting younger people involved in dancing. The Konami Corporation game Dance, Dance Revolution (DDR) has kids of all ages working up a sweat trying to make the moves necessary to win the game.

Research released in 2007 by the West Virginia University School of Medicine's Pediatrics Department found that overweight or obese children who played DDR at home for at least 30 minutes a day, five days a week, maintained their weight rather than adding an average of six pounds – which they did during the first half of the study.[34] An even better side effect was that the kids saw a reduction in some risk factors for heart disease and diabetes. Prior to the study, the children involved reported feeling awkward about going to gym class at school. Afterward, the kids said they felt more confident and willing to try other exercises.

Who would have guessed that a dancing video game might be an answer to America's childhood obesity problem!

Do a Little Dance

For adults with health problems, less strenuous dancing can be very beneficial. Italian researchers have found that waltzing can help chronic heart failure patients – improving heart function, elasticity in their arteries, and quality of life – particularly their emotions.[35] "The problem is that sometimes the adherence of cardiac patients to exercise training programs is not very high, so we have to find something that may capture their interest," Dr. Romualdo Belardinelli, the director of cardiac rehabilitation and prevention at Lancisi Heart Institute in Ancona, Italy, said at an American Heart Association's news conference announcing the results of the study. "Waltz dancing improves functional capacity and quality of life for chronic heart failure patients without important side effects. It may be considered in combination or as an alternative to exercise training in these patients," Belardinelli added.

I always wonder why men, in particular, are so reluctant to dance. Sure, we often do not look as graceful out there as women do, but in my opinion, the benefits far outweigh the risk of looking like a dork. Not only, as mentioned previously, does dancing do your heart and mind good, it has other benefits that are often overlooked.

In the September 2006 issue of *Men's Health* magazine, the results of a study of 800 women were revealed. The women were asked to rate how "hot" men look when they are doing everyday stuff. Dancing well scored a 9-out-of-10, coming in just behind playing with young children.

Wait, it gets better. *Cosmopolitan* magazine teamed up with *Men's Health* to ask 6000 men and women what sort of date best puts them in the mood for sex.[36] Coming in at #2 for the women was a night out dancing (25.4%). For men, dancing finished third (14.6%). Start with a romantic dinner, which finished first for men (27.7%) and third for women (23.4%), and the odds are good you will have a very enjoyable evening.

If you already are light on your feet, get out and enjoy dancing more often. If not, take lessons. Some dances are relatively easy once you learn the steps. Look for a place to take lessons in your area, such as Arthur Murray, or try to find a swing dance club. Members of these clubs are eager to teach others and have regular dance parties.

Go to my Web site, www.BetterSoundAdvice.com, for links to swing dance club sites. You can also find links to online dance instruction sites – just in case you are a little shy and want to learn in the privacy of your home. Nothing, however, beats the experience of learning from someone who knows his or her way around a dance floor. My father is proof of that.

THE ZEN TEN

Songs to get you on the dance floor
(and have fun while you are there)

1. September – Earth Wind & Fire
2. I Want You Back – The Jackson Five
3. Play That Funky Music – Wild Cherry
4. Brown Sugar – The Rolling Stones
5. Jump, Jive, an' Wail – Brian Setzer Orchestra
6. Gonna Make You Sweat – C+C Music Factory
7. The Twist – Chubby Checker
8. Got To Give It Up – Marvin Gaye
9. I Like It, I Love It – Tim McGraw
10. Having A Party – Rod Stewart

* For more, great dance songs, visit www.BetterSoundAdvice. com

Sound Suggestions

Remember These Tips From This Chapter

1. Take dancing lessons.
2. If you have children, encourage them to play Dance, Dance Revolution. Don't be afraid to join in. There is no age limit for DDR.
3. Plan to dance on your next date and then once a month after that.

Notes

I spent a day by the river
It was quiet and the wind stood still
I spent some time with nature
To remind me of all that's real
It's funny how silence speaks sometimes when
you're alone
And remember that you feel
   *– **Creed, Faceless Man***

RELAXING RHYTHM

Do you remember the days when taking a nap was required? In kindergarten, usually right after recess, the teacher had all the children lie down to rest on their nap mats. I am not sure if this quiet time was to calm the children or provide the teacher with a few peaceful minutes, or both, but it was something I always enjoyed.

While some schools have done away with naptime for preschoolers, it would not be a bad idea to bring this practice to the adult world and corporate America. Way back in 1975, Dr. Herbert Benson and his colleagues at the Harvard Medical School published a book called *The Relaxation Response*. It detailed their revolutionary work on how using simple techniques to relax could reduce stress as well as help treat high blood pressure, heart conditions, and insomnia.

The book, which I recommend, instructs people on how to take 10 to 20 minutes out of each day to relax by breathing slowly and loosening up muscles one-by-one to reach the desired effect. To take this one step further, I suggest adding music to this routine. Specifically, slow music with a tempo of around 60 beats per minute. Pachelbel's *Canon in D* seems to be especially effective in helping people relax.

Relax and settle down
Let your mind go round
Lay down on the ground
Listen to the sound of the band
Hold my hand
    – The Who, Relax

Multiple studies have shown that listening to slow, meditative music (usually without any lyrics to distract you) can slow your heart rate, reduce blood pressure[37], and reduce tension in your muscles. The relaxation effect is enhanced with short intervals of silence spaced periodically throughout the listening session. Some scientists believe this type of music therapy could help prevent and/or treat heart disease and stroke.

How does all this apply to corporate America? Well, productivity could get a big boost if workers took a little time each day to relax and, if possible, take a nap.

"No matter how much pressure you feel at work, if you could find ways to relax for at least five minutes every hour, you'd be more productive,"
    – Dr. Joyce Brothers, psychologist

Some of the great leaders of our time believed in the revitalizing capability of power naps. John F. Kennedy, Winston Churchill, Bill Clinton, and Ronald Reagan all scheduled naps into their daily routines. Thomas Edison and Albert Einstein also took frequent naps in the belief it made them more productive, and who's to argue with those two great minds.

ASLEEP ON THE JOB

Recently, the scientists at NASA confirmed what these well-rested men already knew. Naps can improve performance and decision-making. Dr. Mark Rosekind conducted the study while leading the Fatigue Countermeasures Program at the NASA Ames Research Center. Pilots took naps, 26 minutes on average, in the afternoon. The naps boosted performance by 34 percent and improved decision making by 54 percent.[38] Rosekind went on to start a company called Alertness Solutions, a consulting firm that uses information on sleep patterns and alertness to improve productivity and safety in the workplace.

At the University of Haifa in Israel, brain researcher Avi Karni found that daytime naps helped to lock in long-term memories.[39] Participants in the study were able to learn and remember a complex thumb-tapping sequence much more effectively when they took afternoon naps.

Despite the growing amount of evidence that napping can increase productivity, a National Sleep Foundation (NSF) Study found only about 16 percent of companies allow naps at work – and most of those were in the airline, railroad, and hospital industries where accidents caused by a lack of sleep can have severe consequences.

The NSF recommends naps of 20 to 30 minutes to get the most positive effects. Choose a cool, dark, and quiet room to have a restful nap. Mid-afternoon is usually the best time for the nap. Too late in the day can affect your ability to fall asleep at bedtime. You can learn more on the NSF Web site at www.sleepfoundation.org.

Dr. Sara C. Mednick, author of *Take a Nap! Change your life,* says a nap of 15 to 20 minutes will help you feel refreshed and alert because this type of nap contains Stage 2, or REM (Rapid Eye Movement) sleep, which has been shown to improve motor performance and alertness. Longer naps of 30 to 50 minutes can help clear your mind of useless information.

While at Harvard University, Dr. Mednick did a study that found college students performed better on visual tests after taking a nap.[40] The longer the nap, the longer the students were able to perform at a high level. The long nappers also did better at remembering tasks the next day.

Setting up a naptime at work does not necessarily mean rolling out a cot at each worker's desk. Companies like MetroNaps (www.metronaps.com) are putting up nap stations in offices, business districts, and airports all over the world. The nap times (best done about eight hours after awaking from an overnight sleep) should be treated just like coffee breaks. It can help employees and businesses get through those post-lunchtime lulls that are often the least productive times of the day.

I remember well my father coming home from the office each day for a quick lunch and a 20-minute power nap before heading back to work. Dad was a dentist and worked until the age of 78, so the naps sure seemed to help him.

"Your mind will answer most questions if you learn to relax and wait for the answer,"
    – **William S. Burroughs, American Novelist**

A six-year study of Greek adults found those who took midday naps had a 37 percent lower risk of dying from heart disease than those who did not take regular naps.[41] The researchers at the University of Athens Medical School noted the nappers apparently relieved some of the work-related stress that was bad for their hearts.

SOUND WAVES

Even if you find it difficult to fall asleep, taking the time to relax and clear your mind will not only reduce stress, it can help you make better decisions – especially big decisions. By closing your eyes and listening to relaxing music, you effectively refresh or "re-boot" your brain.

What most of us don't realize, or take for granted, is that our brains are constantly monitoring the world around us while we concentrate on the tasks at hand. It filters out what is unimportant but alerts us to what is. This creates a subconscious database of knowledge, which we draw upon, often without realizing it, when making decisions.

Some might refer to this as instinct, gut feeling, or intuition. More often than not, this instinct is right even though we do not know why a certain decision felt right. You do not know how you know, you just know.

This tie between our brains and internal organs is so strong, research has found a new way to determine if a person is lying. When not telling the truth, subjects showed a significant decrease in the percentage of normal gastric "slow waves" in the stomach and a significant increase in the average heart rate. This, combined with the polygraph test, may make lie detectors much more accurate.

In addition, the heart receives and responds to intuitive information. Researchers at HeartMath (www. HeartMath.org) found that we could be aware of an event up to seven seconds before it happens. Subjects in the study had significant changes in heart rate just prior to seeing disturbing images with no knowledge the images would appear.[42] This intuitive sense of danger was stronger, not surprisingly, in women than in men in the study.

Your conscience awakes
And you see your mistakes
And you wish someone
Would buy your confessions.
The days miss their mark
And the night gets so dark
And some kind of message
Comes through to you
Some kind of message
Shoots through
– Dan Fogelberg, Part of the Plan

Ironically, these intuitive powers work better on big decisions than small ones. Say, choosing between colors for bath towels versus choosing which type of car to buy.

A study done at the University of Amsterdam used a process called "deliberation-without-attention" where decisions were left to unconscious thought or "gut feeling." The study found that shoppers viewed their big purchases more favorably when decisions were made without attentive deliberation.[43]

If you take the time to clear your mind before making a big decision, odds are you will be happier with the decision you make.

SHEEP VERSUS SCHUBERT

It used to be that counting sheep was the way people would try to get their minds off their day and help them fall asleep. While not a bad strategy, listening to music is a much better option. Using the same techniques to relax discussed earlier, you can help prepare your brain for sleep prior to bedtime, and the result is a much better night's sleep.

Research done on older patients with sleep disorders showed that those who listened to soft music for 45 minutes prior to going to sleep reported a 35 percent improvement in their sleep disorders. They slept better and longer thanks to the music.

The 2004 study[44], done by Case Western Reserve University's Frances Payne Bolton School of Nursing and the Buddhist Tzu-Chi General Hospital in Taiwan, found that the 30 patients who listened to soft music prior to bed had physical changes, including lower heart and respiratory rates, that helped them get a more restful sleep. The patients also reported less dysfunction the following day.

"Music is pleasant and safe and the technique we used in our study is quick and easy to learn, is low cost, and could be used readily by nurses," Marion Good, professor of nursing at Case Western said. "It is easy to use and does not cause side effects."

> *Golden slumbers fill your eyes*
> *Smiles awake you when you rise*
> *Sleep pretty darling do not cry*
> *And I will sing a lullaby*
> **– The Beatles, Golden Slumbers**

Lullabies worked so well on us when we were babies, why not use them as we grow older? The choice of music should again focus on slow (60 bpm) and meditative songs with few, distracting lyrics. Therefore, while the Rock-a-Bye-Baby lyrics may no longer be appropriate for us, the rhythm of the song certainly is. The 60 beats per minute are key because it closely ties to the average resting heartbeat of humans. If the entrainment effect takes place (where rhythms tend to synchronize), your heart rate will slow to match the beat of the music.

SLEEP AND STRESS

If you can improve your sleep patterns, there is also a good chance you will improve your health. A study at Columbia University's Mailman School of Public Health and the Obesity Research Center found that the less sleep you get the more weight you are likely to gain.[45] Researchers reported that study subjects between the ages of 32 and 59 who got just six hours of sleep per night were 23 percent more likely to be substantially overweight than those who slept between seven and nine hours. With less sleep, the weight increased. Those who got only five hours of sleep were 50 percent more likely to be obese and those who slept four hours or less had a 73 percent chance of being fatter.

Furthermore, a study at the University of Chicago found that the less sleep men got, the higher the levels of cortisol in their blood.[46] Higher levels of cortisol lead to higher levels of stored fat in the body.

Similar results have been found in children. Research at Northwestern University showed that children who get less sleep tend to weigh more five years later.[47] Researchers found that an extra hour of sleep reduced the likelihood of being overweight from 36 percent to 30 percent in children ages 3 to 8, and from 34 percent to 30 percent for those ages 8 to 13.

Not reducing stress by failing to relax during the day compounds the problem even more. When we are under stress, the body produces two hormones: cortisol and adrenaline. This is good when we are fleeing a burning building, since it gives us a boost of energy. It is not so good when we are stressing over a decision at work.

Under stress, we tend to grab high sugar food sources to feed our body's need for fuel. Without running away from the danger, since we are usually just sitting at a desk, the sugar gets stored as fat, and we get heavier.

Research done at Yale University found that people with higher stress-induced levels of cortisol ate more sweets, and more food for that matter, than people with lower levels of cortisol.[48]

So find a way to relax each day, perhaps several times a day, especially when you are stressed. Keep your iPod handy with a playlist of relaxing music, turn down the lights, close your eyes, and listen your stress away.

At night, set aside at least 30 minutes prior to bedtime to listen to relaxing music. Get rid of as many distractions as you can and try not to watch television or read just prior to going to sleep. These tend to have the opposite effect by causing your brain to become active again.

Below is a list of songs that I have found to be effective in helping me relax. You may also consider buying a CD designed specifically for relaxation. You can also visit my Web site, www.BetterSoundAdvice.com to read the suggestions of others or tell us what works best for you.

THE ZEN TEN

Songs that help you relax

1. Orchestral Suite No. 3 in D major, BWV 1068: Air (Bach) – Bach Colleguim Japan & Masaaki Suzuki
2. Flamenco Sketches – Miles Davis
3. Piano Concerto No. 21 in C Major (Mozart) – English Chamber Orchestra
4. Round Midnight – Thelonious Monk

5. Adagio for Strings, Op. 11 (Corelli) – Leonard Bernstein & New York Philharmonic

6. Canon and Gigue for 3 Violins and Basso Continuo in D Major: Canon (Pachelbel) – English Chamber Orchestra

7. I Want To Talk About You – John Coltrane

8. A Midsummer Night's Dream, Op. 61: Nocturne (Mendelssohn) – Royal Philharmonic Orchestra

9. Thaïs: Méditation Religieuse – Symphonie – National Philharmonic Orchestra of London

10. Chant – Music for the Soul – Cistercian Monks of Stift Heiligenkreuz

* For more music to help you relax, visit www.BetterSoundAdvice.com

SOUND SUGGESTIONS

Remember These Tips From This Chapter

1. Use music to relax during breaks at work. It helps reduce stress.

2. Take a mid-day nap when possible to recharge.
3. Play relaxing music (60 beats per minute) 30 minutes prior to bedtime.
4. Use this last part of your day to clear your mind.

Keep a notepad by your bed and before going to sleep remember to put your thoughts on paper. I refer to this as getting Out of Your Mind!® The word MIND is an acronym for the following:

Most Important Task. This is the one thing you must do the next day. There can only be one most important task and list it here.

Ideas that you have that you want to pursue. Write them down so you don't forget them!

Next to do list. This is a list of the other goals you have for the next day, week or month. You can work on these after you finish your most important task.

Daily Reflection/Affirmations. Write down your thoughts about what you accomplished that day. Reinforce the positive things that occurred. Take the time to write a thank you note to someone that helped you today or in the past. It will make them and you feel better.

Notes

When I was younger, so much younger than today,
I never needed anybody's help in any way.
But now these days are gone, I'm not so self assured,
Now I find I've changed my mind and opened up
the doors.

Help me if you can, I'm feeling down
And I do appreciate you being round.
Help me get my feet back on the ground,
Won't you please, please help me?
   *– **The Beatles, Help!***

LYRICAL INSPIRATION

In the fall of 1965, a little radio station in Evansville, Indiana (WJPS-A.M.) introduced a new technology that allowed listeners to call in and record anything they wanted to ask or say to the DJ. Sometimes the DJ played back for the audience what was recorded, other times he did not.

What I recorded that day made it on the air only a few minutes after the call. I sang the song *Help!* by The Beatles, word-for-word, all the way to the end. Only nine-years-old at the time, the lyrics hit home with me, and I felt the need to express them. Many people probably heard my off-key rendition, but I am not sure how many were really listening or understood why I sang them.

John Lennon wrote the song after having feelings of being overwhelmed by the enormous popularity of The Beatles – and the fact he found himself eating and drinking too much.

I connected with the lyrics for a much different reason. Two years earlier, at age 7 and just one week after the assassination of President John F. Kennedy, my mom died of breast cancer. I can still remember my father gathering my brothers and sisters in his bedroom that November night and mustering up the courage to tell us "the angels came today and took your mother to heaven."

I was devastated. While only seven, I was old enough to know what this meant. I would never see her again.

Back then, there was not much doctors could do for breast cancer. Moreover, when someone died, you did not talk about it in front of children.

Despite still having my father, five sisters, and two brothers, I felt terribly alone. My dad had lots of friends who did a wonderful job of helping us when they could, but there was no replacing my mom. She was gone, and there was a big, empty space in my life.

I am sure my entire family felt much the same way. My dad, a wonderful man, had to work incredibly hard to keep building his dental practice while still trying to take care of his eight children. His heart was surely broken by his wife's death, but he never showed it – at least in front of us kids. He was too busy providing for us.

Two years later, the movie *Help!* came to town. I grabbed some coins I had saved up and walked downtown to the movie theater by myself. It probably was not the smartest thing I ever did. It was a good three miles, and I had to walk through an area of town that had been experiencing some racial tension (this was the mid-60s), but I was determined to see the movie. Afterwards, I couldn't wait to hear the song again, over and over again. Those words kept ringing in my head.

"And now my life has changed in oh so many ways,
My independence seems to vanish in the haze.
But every now and then I feel so insecure,
I know that I just need you like I've never done before."
 – The Beatles, Help!

It was as if Lennon had written the song about my life. I needed my mom like I'd never done before. Repeating the lyrics did not change that, but somehow it gave me comfort – maybe comfort in knowing that others in the world felt the same way sometimes. From that day on, I started listening closely to the words in songs, looking for other phrases that would comfort or inspire me.

EYEWITNESS NEWS

The 1960s were not easy on our family. It seemed to me I was always at the funeral home. My mom's father died only a few months before she did. Her older sister had died of cancer two years earlier. In 1965, my dad's father passed away. Then, two years later, another tragedy struck.

My Uncle Bill, my mom's brother, made extra money during the Christmas season playing Santa Claus. I had seen him a number of times dressed up as jolly old St. Nick. That December 1967, Uncle Bill was to be part of a holiday promotion at a local shopping center. Santa Claus would be making a special appearance for the children and would arrive by helicopter.

What no one expected was that some power lines at the edge of the shopping center parking lot would catch part of the helicopter on its way in. The helicopter flipped over and crashed into the ground, killing both the pilot and Santa Claus – my Uncle Bill.

Hundreds of children who witnessed the crash were in shock, asking their parents if Santa Claus was really dead. I lost an uncle that day, his family lost a wonderful husband and father, and those children who saw it probably would never forget the day Santa died.

So there I was at the funeral home again – wondering why these things happen. I kept wondering every time things like this occurred in my life.

In 1970, I was a passenger in a school bus coming back from a high school football game. The bus was struck head on by a car. Two kids, on a joy ride in a stolen car, died instantly. I was lucky to have only a busted lip and a few scrapes and scratches. The image of the car with the two dead boys inside is still etched in my memory.

In 1977, while working at the Evansville airport, I was an eyewitness to a plane crash. The plane was carrying the University of Evansville basketball team. All 29 people on board died.

I grew up watching this team. The university was only a few blocks from my home, and I used to walk over to the gym and sneak in to watch practice. One of the players even gave me an old game jersey to keep. I treasured it for years. The plane crash was another blow to a part of my childhood.

The night of the crash and the next day, I ended up being interviewed by newspapers, radio stations, and television reporters from across the country, including the *CBS Evening News with Walter Cronkite.*

SOUND BITES

I am not sure if all this news coverage led me to that profession or not, but I ended up spending the 1980s as a television reporter and anchor. Over the next 11 years, I reported on more tragedies and deaths than I can possibly remember. On the outside, my emotions rarely showed when reporting on those events, but inside there was still a deep hurt and longing for what I still missed so much – my mom.

During this 20-year span, my music collection continued to grow, and I spent hours of my free time making cassette tapes of my favorite songs to listen to while driving, when I needed a little inspiration, or for just working around the house.

I had a knack for putting together compilations that had meaning and flowed well. In college, most any party sponsored by my fraternity featured my music tapes. Friends recognized this talent and asked me to record tapes for them. I even had a few gigs as a DJ at reunions and weddings.

My key to success involved really listening to the lyrics and watching closely how music affected people. I knew how to have a song tie to an event, how to get people on the dance floor and keep them there, and how to find the right song to fit almost any mood. More importantly, however, I found songs that would comfort or inspire me when I needed it.

When I find myself in times of trouble
Mother Mary comes to me
Speaking words of wisdom, let it be
And in my hour of darkness
She is standing right in front of me
Speaking words of wisdom, let it be
Let it be, let it be
   *– **The Beatles, Let It Be***

These tapes and CDs came in handy when the cancer gene that caused my mother's death started to affect her children.

In 1996, my older sister was diagnosed with the same type of breast cancer our mother had. Three years later, one of my younger sisters was diagnosed with thyroid cancer after it had spread to several lymph nodes. Then, in October 2001, just a few weeks after the 9-11 terrorist attacks, I was diagnosed with thyroid cancer.

Right after my surgery, I compiled a new CD to listen to titled, "Radioactive Rock" in honor of the radioactive iodine treatments I would undergo to kill the cancer cells inside my body. The CD was upbeat, inspiring, and kept me going when I felt a little weak or tired.

While there were some scary moments for my sisters and myself, I don't think any of us had any doubt we would survive these cancers – and we have. All three of us are cancer free at this time.

I attribute this to a couple of things.

First, I firmly believe that somewhere out there our mother is helping to watch over us. Perhaps when we did need her like we've "never done before," she was there for us.

Second, a positive attitude. Yes, despite everything I have been through in my life, I have mostly had a positive outlook on life. Most of my siblings are the same way.

"Everything can be taken from a man or a woman but one thing: the last of human freedoms to choose one's attitude in any given set of circumstances, to choose one's own way,"
    – Viktor Frankel, Psychiatrist, Author and former Nazi concentration camp prisoner

SOUNDS GOOD

Our father may have something to do with this outlook. A deeply religious man, he set a very good example for us. He always talked about the good things in our lives and never dwelled on the bad.

Even recently, when some good friends of the family – one of those who did so much to help us when mom died – had a daughter dying of cancer, Dad found a way to talk about the positive. While I was thinking about how her situation compared to the death of my mom, my dad's comment was, "You know, we've been pretty lucky."

The statement took me by surprise. I thought for certain it would cause him to think about mom's death. Instead he said, "We've all been fortunate, my kids are all healthy. You, Mary Beth and Jane have all survived your cancers. We've been blessed."

I couldn't help but agree and had an even bigger appreciation for how he continues to live his life with a positive attitude.

Why I am telling you all this? Well, certainly not for your sympathy. I feel pretty good about my life and consider myself fortunate in many ways. I am telling you this because I believe no matter how bad things seem to be, a positive attitude can make all the difference. Moreover, if you can find it through the lyrics of a song – all the better.

*You probably don't want to hear advice from
someone else
But I wouldn't be telling you if I hadn't been there
myself
It's alright, it's alright
Sometimes that's all it takes
We're only human
We're supposed to make mistakes*
   – Billy Joel, You're Only Human

Billy Joel wrote *You're Only Human*, a very upbeat and positive number, to inspire teenagers who might be contemplating suicide. His inspiration came from the fact that Joel tried to kill himself at the young age of 21 by drinking a bottle of furniture polish.

"I sat on a chair waiting to die and then thought, this is sick," Joel was quoted as saying.[49] A friend rushed Joel to the hospital and saved his life. Joel then got professional help.

This is one of many songs that I play on occasion to pick me up. It can help you stay positive even on the darkest days.

Why should you listen to me, my dad, Billy Joel, or any of the other people quoted in this book?

Because research shows staying positive will help you live a longer, happier life.

P O S I T I V E   R E S U L T S

Dr. Barbara Fredrickson did research to help prove this theory. She was awarded the first-ever Templeton

Prize in Positive Psychology[50] after proving that positive emotions can actually help undo the damage done to the cardiovascular system by negative emotions. Fredrickson is currently a psychology professor at the University of North Carolina.

Think about that. Stress and negative emotions actually do damage to us internally – causing, among other things, stomach ulcers, hypertension, and respiratory illnesses. The longer you live life as a pessimist, the shorter that life is likely to be.

In The Netherlands, a study on attitude and health produced some surprising results. Researchers followed nearly one thousand Dutch subjects between the ages of 65 and 85 for ten years.[51] Those subjects with the highest levels of optimism were 45 percent *less likely* to die during the study than those with the highest levels of pessimism. The researchers attributed much of the optimist's longevity to the prevention of cardiovascular mortality, while the pessimists may have been suffering from undiagnosed depression, which has been linked to higher rates of heart disease. In addition, the optimists may have done a better job of dealing with adversity and engaging in healthy activities.

Being a naysayer, a pessimist, and/or a depressed person is unhealthy and it might kill you. Yet, finding the good in situations and people, being positive and happy may improve your health. So why would you not work on trying to stay positive and to be happy?

For more proof, you can read about the work done at the Institute of HeartMath. Its scientists have used "designer music" and self-induced positive emotional states to actually enhance the body's immune system. The combination resulted in a 140 percent increase in production of salivary IgA, the first line of defense in the human body's immune system when attacked by viruses or microbes.[52]

Other research has shown that as much as 35 percent of the effect of medical treatment is the belief of the patients in the doctor and the treatment given them.[53] I never once thought my cancer would kill me. I knew I would beat this disease. Whether that attitude made a difference, I don't know. Nevertheless, it certainly did not hurt me in any way to have those beliefs.

Our dominant thoughts influence our body without known physiological connections. If you believe you will get better, it increases the chances you will. You may also live longer with a positive attitude. A study of older residents in Oxford, Ohio found that those with a positive view of aging lived seven and a half years longer than those who did not.[54]

Here's hoping all the days ahead
Won't be as bitter as the ones behind you.
Be an optimist instead,
And somehow happiness will find you.
Forget what happened yesterday,
I know that better things are on the way.
  *– **The Kinks, Better Things***

GETTING BETTER EVERY DAY

Research at the University of Chicago found that executives who saw downsizing as a personal threat had more than a 90 percent chance of becoming severely ill during or soon after the downsizing. Less than a third of the executives who had a positive attitude became ill.[55]

Still more research shows that people with a positive attitude do better in school, at work, and at home. They are usually healthier – both physically and mentally. They rarely get depressed and are more likely to take care of themselves. In addition, when they do get sick, they recover faster than pessimists do.[56]

If you are looking for a job, a huge majority of hiring managers say a positive, enthusiastic attitude is the most appealing behavior you can show during an interview.[57]

> *Into this life we're born*
> *Baby sometimes we don't know why*
> *And time seems to go by so fast*
> *In the twinkling of any eye.*
> *Let's enjoy it while we can*
> *Won't you help me sing my song*
> *From the dark end of the street*
> *To the bright side of the road*
> * – **Van Morrison**, Bright Side Of The Road*

Van Morrison does not have the best reputation on tour. He is reported to be moody and temperamental. He was the first living artist inducted into the Rock and Roll Hall of Fame who did not attend his induction ceremony. His music, however, can be very inspiring.

A visionary who has explored various styles of music and once expressed interest in teaching philosophy at Belfast University, Morrison creates lyrics that are both introspective and spiritual. *Whenever God Shines His*

Light on Me and *Bright Side of the Road* are both examples of this. When I listen to *Bright Side of the Road,* it always seems to put me in a good mood.

Another of my favorite positive songs is the closing song from the Monty Python movie, *Life of Brian.*

> *If life seems jolly rotten*
> *There's something you've forgotten*
> *And that's to laugh and smile and dance and sing.*
> *When you're feeling in the dumps*
> *Don't be silly chumps*
> *Just purse your lips and whistle - that's the thing.*
> *And...always look on the bright side of life...*
> *Always look on the light side of life...*
> **– Eric Idle, Monty Python, Always Look on the Bright Side Of Life**

Eric Idle wrote this song to make light of the moment at the end of the movie when a number of prisoners, including the lead character, Brian, are being crucified. It has since, according to Idle, become one of the top-10 songs played at funerals. If it can cheer people up at a funeral, imagine how effective it can be when you are feeling a bit depressed.

> *I'm gonna stop looking back start moving on*
> *And learn how to face my fears*
> *Love with all of my heart make my mark*
> *I wanna leave something here*
> *Go out on a ledge without any net*
> *That's what I'm gonna be about*
> *Yeah, I wanna be running when the sand runs out*
> **– Rascal Flatts, When The Sand Runs Out**

SOUND DECISIONS

Speaking of funerals, the message behind the Rascal Flatts song, *When the Sand Runs Out*, centers around the death of a man's best friend and how it inspired living life to the fullest.

A life-changing event is what causes many people to take steps to improve the way they live. For me, it was being diagnosed with cancer. I exercised occasionally prior to my diagnosis but afterward, I started hitting the gym four or five days a week and have not stopped since.

See the moon roll across the stars
See the seasons turn like a heart
Your father's days are lost to you
This is your time here to do what you will do
Your life is now your life is now your life is now
 – John Mellencamp, Your Life is Now

It is too bad it takes a health problem, the death of someone close to us, or another type of loss to cause us to change.

That was the case with John Mellencamp when he wrote *Your Life Is Now*. He had suffered a heart attack at age 42, and realized he was tired of living his life on the road. "And then I decided that I was really wasting an opportunity and that I needed to refocus my life," Mellencamp told the *Seattle Post-Intelligencer* in 1999. "My wife had a lot to do with changing my outlook. It was like when somebody looks at you and they say, 'You know, you're an idiot for thinking like that.'"[58]

Why doesn't everyone have this attitude – trying to run until the sand runs out, knowing your life is now? Probably because we don't slow down long enough to realize how fast life is passing us by.

> *And you run and you run to catch up with the sun, but it's sinking*
> *Racing around to come up behind you again*
> *The sun is the same in a relative way, but you're older*
> *Shorter of breath and one day closer to death*
> *Every year is getting shorter never seem to find the time*
> **– Pink Floyd, Time**

An Associated Press poll in the spring of 2006 found Americans are an inpatient lot. More than half of us get antsy if we are on hold for more than five minutes or in line for more than 15 minutes. This causes anger and, as has been proven repeatedly, anger causes health problems.

> *Try to realize it's all within yourself*
> *no one else can make you change*
> *And to see you're really only very small*
> *and life flows on within you and without you*
> **– George Harrison, Within You Without You**

The first step in making a change in your life – anger management, losing weight, spending more time with your family, or pursuing a new career – is writing down your intentions and setting a goal. When you have an intention, it drives the brain to generate action. If you have a written goal, that action is more likely to result in an achievement.

> *Make a promise, take a vow*
> *And trust your feelings, it's easy now.*
> *Understand the voice within*
> *And feel the changes already beginning*
> *– **The Moody Blues, The Voice***

S O U N D   G O A L S

Thinking about your goals is good. Stating them aloud, on a regular basis, is even better.

You have probably heard about the study on goals and the Harvard University Class of 1979.[59] When the graduates were surveyed, only 16 percent had clear goals for their future – and only 3 percent had taken the time to write down the goals and plans to achieve them.

Ten years later, the 13 percent with goals were earning twice as much as the 84 percent with no goals. Even more impressive was that the 3 percent with written goals were earning almost eleven times as much as the other 97 percent of the class.

The message to set goals and write them down is clear. Research that is more recent shows that verbalizing and visualizing your goals will improve your chances of reaching them.

In your head is the answer
Let it guide you along
Let your heart be the anchor
And the beat of your own song
You don't get something for nothing
You can't have freedom for free
   – Rush, Something For Nothing

Tiger Woods, arguably the best golfer in the world right now and perhaps the greatest of all time, credits much of his success to his father getting him to visualize what he wanted to achieve.

Tiger often talks about how his father, Earl, told him to "putt to the picture" and it was the best advice on putting he ever received. "I get a picture in my head and stroke the ball toward what I see in the picture while keeping my head perfectly still," Tiger says on his official Web site, www.tigerwoods.com.

Two different sports studies have found that if athletes talk to themselves aloud, it will improve their performance. Positive, descriptive words, such as "I can accomplish anything" worked best. This was most effective during practice and not in actual competition.

Hold on to your dream
Cause they're always worth having
Hold on to your dream
Like a mother to her child
Don't let anyone ever steal your dreams from you
Hold on to your dream
And do your best to always wear a smile
   – Stevie Wonder, Hold On To Your Dream

I am not suggesting you begin talking to yourself while sitting in the office. Your co-workers might start to wonder about you. Instead, write down your goals and post them in a place, or places, you see every day. Then, occasionally, read one of your goals out loud. This can be in the morning while getting ready for work or during the drive to or from the office.

Once you write down and state your goals, your brain then helps to shape the actions needed to fit your goals. This "cognitive control," as neuroscientists refer to it, helps you start to act in a way that will move you toward your goals. The more you focus on the acts needed to reach your goals, the more your brain gets actively involved.

When you have a stressful day, and your goals seem a little farther away, take time to write about that stress and how you are feeling. Not only can putting the words to paper help clear your mind, it can help you feel better. A study at the State University of New York at Stony Brook found that patients undergoing medical treatment showed marked improvement when they wrote about the feelings surrounding a stressful event in their lives.[60] Nearly half (47 percent) of those in the study showed improvement compared to 24 percent of those who simply wrote about their plans for the day.

I own my insecurities
I try to own my destiny
That I can make or break it if I choose
   – Sarah McLachlan, Perfect Girl

There is one additional obstacle, however, that you will have to overcome. The thought that you cannot reach your goal – the fear of failure.

A study by American Express found that 52 percent of British people have a dream they would like to pursue but half said fear is the main thing holding them back.[61] I suspect the research would produce similar results if done in America or most any other country.

Humans have a tendency to choose the safer option, even though the chance for reward is lower than choosing a risky option with a higher potential payoff. This may be easy to do when choosing between the $5 and the $100 black jack tables in Las Vegas. It is a little more difficult when the risk is your career.

When trying to make a big decision, many people make it more difficult by thinking about the decision too much. I am not suggesting to forego doing your due diligence first, but as discussed earlier, often your gut instinct is the best way to go.

> *Take the straight and narrow path*
> *And if you start to slide*
> *Give a little whistle! Give a little whistle!*
> *And always let your conscience be your guide*
> *– **Jiminy Cricket, Give a Little Whistle***

SOUNDS RIGHT

Yet more wisdom from a Disney movie, ***Pinocchio***. Jiminy Cricket, whose name is also a euphemism for Jesus Christ, has the title of "Lord High Keeper of the Knowledge of Right and Wrong, Counselor in Moments of Temptation, and Guide along the Straight and

Narrow Path." Most of us remember him as Pinocchio's conscience.

This "voice within," as the conscience is often referred to in philosophical terms, is a human's ability to discern between right and wrong. Whether this is an innate ability or is a result of life's experience is debatable. In either case, letting your conscience be your guide is good advice.

And a new day will dawn for those
Who stand long . . .
Yes there are two paths you can go by.
But in the long run.
There's still time to change the road you're on.
   – Led Zeppelin, Stairway To Heaven

Are there risks in making life-changing decisions? Of course. Is there a chance of failure? Absolutely. More than 1,400 climbers have scaled Mount Everest, and some 180 people have died trying.[62] Yet, each year, despite a greater than 10 percent chance of dying, more people try to reach the top of the world. You rarely succeed at anything great without first taking a chance.

A study in the *Journal of Business Strategies* found that risk-taking had a positive relation to the performance of businesses[63]. In addition, the more stable and predictable the business environment, the more risk-taking may be fruitful, according to the study's authors. It's often the competitive advantage needed to set your company apart from the rest.

I have never considered myself a risk taker. You will not see me skydiving, betting huge sums of money on a roll of the dice, or running with scissors. However, I have taken some risks in my life and most have paid off.

One of the biggest risks was quitting my job as a television reporter/anchor to start a sports newspaper from scratch. I had a wife and two small children at the time, and failure was not an option. The thought of not being able to make my mortgage payments or feed my family almost caused me to play it safe with my TV job, even though I was not very happy.

My friend, Tim, then said something to me that convinced me to go for it. In a twist on the old "better to have tried and failed" quote, he said, "You will be better off, and earn more respect, by trying to start your own business and failing than never having tried at all."

He was right. I knew that even if I did not make this business work, I had enough confidence in my abilities to make something work eventually. It was worth the risk to find a career that would make me happy rather than stay stuck in my current situation.

See the future in the past
Try to change or make it last
Go for broke don't regret
Get your hands dirty get your feet wet
Take your place use me well
I'm in your hands so make me tell
A broken dream seems unkind
But I can help for I am time
  *– **The Moody Blues, The Spirit***

Statistics show that a little less than 1-in-5 entrepreneurs are successful in their first venture. That success ratio goes up by 2 percent with the next venture. In addition, if they follow a proven formula, such as a franchise system, the success ratio more than triples.

Thankfully, the business I helped to start made it and did very well. I sold it seven years later at a handsome profit. I was a little lucky, but most of the success I can attribute to research, to hard work, and to surrounding myself with good people – particularly my friends and business partners, Bill and Alan.

Sound Principles

Courage, often referred to as the eighth virtue, seems to be lacking in our society today. As with the Cowardly Lion in *The Wizard of Oz*, many of us are "victims of disorganized thinking," often brought on by a lack of confidence.

It is not easy to lose weight, start a new career, or even stand in the face of danger. Courage could be defined as willingly doing something, which would normally be avoided, for the greater good of yourself and others.

'Cause when push comes to shove
You taste what you're made of
You might bend 'til you break
'Cause it's all you can take
On your knees you look up
Decide you've had enough
You get mad, you get strong
Wipe your hands, shake it off
Then you stand, then you stand
*– **Rascal Flatts, Stand***

Courage can be as simple as having the confidence and competence to perform when the situation demands it.

Not long after I had sold my business, I had taken a job as a sales manager in the insurance industry. Less than a year after I took the job, the company announced it was merging with another and there was a good chance I would lose my job.

A few months before the merger was to become final, all the company sales managers gathered for our annual meeting. I decided to participate in a presentation called "best practices." This is where the sales people share the ideas that work for them to increase sales.

I decided to go a little different route. My talk centered on how, in a business where you hear a lot of negative comments, I stayed positive. I shared the story of my mom dying, my sisters and my cancer diagnosis, and how I will probably be out of a job when the merger was complete. With all that, I said I did not complain about it to my clients, friends, or family. I told them my positive attitude would carry me through it all, and I then read them this line from The Eagles song, *Already Gone*:

"So often times it happens that we live our lives in chains And we never even know we have the key"

I shared with them that this line is at the end of every e-mail message I send. From what I have seen in my lifetime, it is a very profound lyric.

Too many people live as if they are in a self-made prison. They complain about their lives, their situations, how others have wronged them . . . the list goes on forever. Yet, they never take the time to get up off their butt and do something about it. It is too easy to blame someone or something else.

They choose to ignore the stories of other people who have beaten the odds or overcome great obstacles or handicaps to become successful and happy. Those stories invariably contain the ingredients of hard work and courage in spite of the dangers involved.

I frequently get comments from people about that tagline in my e-mails. Some are from people who just happen to be Eagles fans. Others, who remark about how true or profound that line is, are often people I consider successful. They understand that you cannot truly be great unless you free yourself from the chains of negativity and pursue your dreams.

"You must be the change you wish to see in the world,"
   – Mahatma Gandhi

It took a little courage for me to give that speech. I was more nervous than I usually am when speaking in front of groups (and I've done it many times) because I was revealing such personal information and challenging my peers to become better people.

When finished, I got a standing ovation. A few people were even crying, and they told me how much I had touched them emotionally. I also won an award for one of the top presentations. More importantly, however, was that one of those in the audience was so impressed with my talk that she hired me. I no longer had to worry about not having a job, and I would not have had one since my old job fell victim to the merger – all because I had the confidence and competence to perform when the situation demanded.

Well I just heard the news today
It seems my life is going to change
I closed my eyes, begin to pray
Then tears of joy stream down my face
With arms wide open
Under the sunlight
Welcome to this place
I'll show you everything
With arms wide open
   – Creed, With Arms Wide Open

Sound Off

Many of us hear the "voice within" but how we follow through on what our conscience tells us may depend more on the development of our moral virtues. Do we have the courage to do the right thing despite what others may be saying or doing?

While our instincts and a little bravery can aid us in times of physical danger to ourselves or someone close to us, courage when confronted with an ethical issue is often far more difficult. Do you look the other way when you see people doing unethical or immoral behavior? Or do you take a stand?

Confronting these situations might best be called moral courage, and it is something we need more of in today's society. Many of the recent, major scandals in this country (Enron, Steroids in sports, Duke Lacrosse team) could have been prevented or made less of an issue if someone had the moral courage to speak up early on.

There is very little chance you will ever be faced with an ethical dilemma of that magnitude. Still, would you confront the co-worker stealing from the company? The friend who is cheating on their spouse? Would you be the lone soldier standing against an army of tanks when you know what is being done is wrong?

Would you teach your children to tell the truth
Would you take the high road if you could choose
Do you believe you're a victim of a great
compromise
'Cause I believe you could change your mind and
change our lives
   – John Mellencamp, Your Life is Now

Knowing when the time is right for you to display moral courage is not always apparent. You must weigh the risks versus the rewards.

I know I have not always displayed moral courage when I should have and, in some cases, I have regretted it. The times when I have spoken up, I felt very good about what happened.

One of the toughest was years ago when stories were circling through my group of friends that my best friend's girlfriend had cheated on him. No one wanted to tell him in fear it would upset him too much. My feelings were just the opposite. I thought he needed to know right away before their relationship progressed any further.

When I told my friend about the cheating, he did get upset but, thankfully, not at me. He immediately confronted his girlfriend, found out the rumors were true, and they broke up. My friend then called a girl he always wanted to ask on a date. They eventually got married and today have a wonderful family.

Having the courage to tell my friend what had happened was not easy. What happened as a result of that was well worth the risk I took.

Lean on me
When you're not strong
I'll be your friend
I'll help you carry on
For.....it won't be long
Till I'm gonna need
Somebody to lean on
  – Bill Withers, Lean On Me

A good friend of mine refers to this as "making a withdrawal from our relationship bank." In other words, if you have built a trusting friendship you should have the right to be brutally honest without fear of destroying that relationship. Those are true friendships, and I treasure the ones I have like that.

The risk can be a little greater when you try to get up the nerve to say something to someone who is not a friend.

SOUND RESULTS

The other incident from my past I want to share involved saying something bold to somcone I barely knew.

As you read earlier in this book, my mom died when I was young. After she passed away, few people talked to me about her or her death. I think they were afraid of making me upset. What they did not know is that I desperately wanted to hear everything I could about my mom. What was she like? What were her talents? What did she think about me?

The few times someone did talk to me about Mom, I listened intently and can remember those conversations almost word-for-word to this day.

Recently, at my high school reunion, I ran into a man who was married to one of my classmates. The woman, Monica, had died of cancer a few months before the reunion. She left behind her husband and two children.

While many people were offering their condolences to this man, I could not help but think of my situation growing up. While I probably had no right to do so, I spoke up and told this man my feelings and what I felt he should do to help his kids remember their mom.

I did not think much more about this conversation until a few weeks later when one of my good friends and fellow classmates forwarded me an e-mail. Apparently, the man I spoke with had been sending updates to friends and family on how he and the children were coping with Monica's death. The e-mail my friend forwarded had quite an impact on me. Here is that e-mail:

Rick,
I don't know if you've been receiving these, but I thought that you might be interested in reading this one. You're the best!!! KK

In a message, ****@****.net writes:

We are talking about Monica every day and that is good. We are past the point where it hurts too much to remember the good and funny times and that makes us all feel good. I was scared about how I was going to deal with that part of things, when and how much to talk about Monica and I kept praying for the wisdom to make good choices. I went to the pre-reunion get together in Evansville for Monica's 30th high school reunion when we were there in July. I was concerned that I would not be able to stand a full night of condolences but it was very good for all of us. I met so many people that needed to talk to me about Monica and express their feelings that it was a great time and I ended up staying until the place closed down. A guy came by and we talked and he said he remembered me from previous reunions. He talked about Monica and it was obvious he had a lot more to say besides that and told me to listen carefully to him. He shared that he had lost his Mom when he was 7 and that family and friends were scared to talk about her when he was around and all he wanted to hear were stories about his Mom. He told me, talk to them, tell them stories, remember everything you can and keep talking about her as the kids will really want to hear everything you can tell. Once again, God gave me His answer.

Needless to say, I shed a few tears when I read that. Never did I imagine that my words could have that kind of effect on someone. It gave me a good feeling inside. The reward was much greater than the risk.

This was far from a situation where I was putting my life at risk, but it did take a little courage to say those things. I hope that it will be a life-changing event for this man and his children. I know it was for me.

> *It's a beautiful day, the sky falls*
> *And you feel like it's a beautiful day*
> *It's a beautiful day*
> *Don't let it get away*
> *– U2, **Beautiful Day***

Now, I am not encouraging you or anyone else to begin stopping strangers to give them advice. If a parent wants to yell at their children in the middle of a crowded grocery store, that one is probably best left alone. There will come times, however, when you get that gut feeling that you need to speak up, or stand up and be counted, or be the one to change your mind and change someone's life – maybe even yours.

A recent study found that one in four Americans have no close friends they can trust to discuss personal matters.[64] Even more of a concern is that our circle of friends is shrinking. Americans are becoming more socially isolated. What a shame.

SOUND CONCLUSIONS

The purpose of this book is to show you how you can use music to improve your life. It is not to encourage you to walk around every waking hour of the day with your iPod and earbuds plugged in, isolating yourself from the rest of the world.

Use music when it can do the most good: while exercising, dancing, relaxing, etc. The rest of the time, get out and be with people. Make new friends. Develop trusting relationships. Spend quality time with people you care for. Humans need to be around other humans. The social interaction and involvement in the community helps us live longer, happier, more fulfilling lives.

Use what you can from this book to improve your life. Set a goal. Choose lyrics that help inspire you. Get out and dance. In making your life better, you will be surprised how this helps improve the lives of those around you. Focus on no "Garbage In" so there is no "Garbage Out." Eliminate the garbage you hear and see, and instead fill your brain with positive sounds, images, and feelings. The output will be much better as a result.

Use my personal mantra, if you would like. I read these words every morning:

"Stay Positive. Make Good Decisions. Do The Right Thing."

You have the key to unlock the chains of your life. That key is **YOU**. Remember, your life is now, so get busy living it!

THE ZEN TEN

Lines from songs to inspire

1. There's still time to change the road you're on.
2. Hold onto your dream.
3. Make a promise, take a vow. And trust your feelings, it's easy now
4. Always let your conscience be your guide.
5. You're only human, you're allowed to make your share of mistakes.
6. It's a beautiful day. Don't let it get away.
7. I wanna be running when the sand runs out.
8. Always look on the bright side of life.
9. So often times it happens that we live our lives in chains and we never even know we have the key.
10. This is your time here to do what you will do. Your life is now.

* For more inspirational lyrics, visit www.BetterSoundAdvice.com

SOUND SUGGESTIONS

Remember These Tips From This Chapter

1. Write down song lyrics that inspire or strike a chord with you. Use them as your personal mantra.
2. Listen to positive songs to help rid yourself of negative emotions.
3. Say something positive to someone else every day.
4. Write down your goals every night. Visualize these goals being realized.
5. Trust your gut instinct when making big decisions.
6. When the time is right, speak up for what you believe in.
7. Make Family, Friends, and Fun an important part of your daily life.

Notes

♫

THE ZEN TEN

Recommended books on music and life

1. The Power Of Sound – Joshua Leeds
2. The Healing Power Of Sound – Mitchell L. Gaynor, M.D.
3. Music, The Brain, And Ecstasy – Robert Jourdain
4. This Is Your Brain On Music – Daniel Levitin
5. Life's Greatest Lessons – Hal Urban
6. Attitude Is Everything – Keith Harrell
7. How To Win Friends & Influence People – Dale Carnegie
8. How To Stop Worrying And Start Living – Dale Carnegie
9. Success Through A Positive Mental Attitude – Napoleon Hill and W. Clement Stone
10. The Tao of Music, *Sound Psychology* – John M. Ortiz, Ph.D.

ABOUT THE AUTHOR

Rick Notter has over three decades of experience as a writer, public speaker and television personality. As an entrepreneur, he started three successful businesses and sold all at a significant profit.

Rick has won awards on his writing and reporting from: *The Associated Press, The Society of Professional Journalists, The Radio and Television News Directors Association, The College Sports Publishers Association, The Indiana Psychological Association, and The Indiana Dietetic Association.* He has received numerous honors for his achievements in sales and business as well.

Rick is an avid student of music, psychology, business, sales, motivation and technology. *Sound Advice* is the result of years of research on music and the effects it has on humans.

As a professional speaker, Rick has presented to groups ranging from several people to several thousand on a variety of topics including motivation, technology, sales, the art of the interview, and effective listening. His talks are upbeat, energetic and inspiring. He gives his audience techniques and strategies they can use to their advantage in the workplace and at home.

Rick lives with his wife, Mary, in Bloomington, Indiana. He is active in the community having served as a consultant and board member to a number of organizations, including the local YMCA. He is currently Director of Sales for a Fortune 35 company, where he is involved in training and motivating salespeople from all walks of life.

BIBLIOGRAPHY

1 "What Life Means to Einstein: An Interview by George Sylvester Viereck," from *The Saturday Evening Post*. October 26, 1929

2 Associated Press Online, No Cure for Songs Stuck in Your Head; October 20, 2003, http://www.freerepublic.com/focus/f-news/1004513/posts

3 Morning Edition (NPR); Brain researchers are closer to figuring out why some songs get stuck in our head; March 14, 2005

4 Michael McDonald, Rockin' Down the Highway DVD, The Wildlife Concert by The Doobie Brothers, 1996.

5 Britt, Robert Roy, Music Tickles Strong Memories, May 26, 2005, http://www.livescience.com/health/050526_music_memory.html

6 Barrow, Karen, At 60, He Learned to Sing So He Could Learn To Talk, *New York Times*, April 22, 2008

7 Switch off TV and switch on your memory, Reuters News Service; August 28, 2006, http://www.smh.com.au/news/mind-matters/switch-off-tv-switch-on-your-memory/2006/08/30/1156816949023.html

8 Weinberger, Norman M., Music and the Brain; *Scientific American*, October 25, 2004,

9 Choi, Charles Q.,Playing Music Makes You Smart, March 19, 2007, http://www.livescience.com/health/070319_music_brainstem.html

10 College-Bound Seniors National Report: Profile of SAT Program Test Takers. Princeton, NJ: The College Entrance Examination Board, 2001

11 Ghosh, Pallab, Music 'aids the healing process'; BBC News, July 19, 2006

12 Bittman, B., *Medical Science Monitor*, February 2005; vol 11. News release, Giles Communications.

13   *British Medical Journal*, doi:10.1136/bmj.38705.470590.55, December 23, 2005

14   Milliman , Ronald E., Using Background Music to Affect the Behavior of Supermarket Shoppers, *Journal of Marketing*, Vol. 46, No. 3, 1982

15   Lewis, Scott, Sound advice; *Restaurants & Institutions*; April 3, 1991;

16   Rosenfeld, Anne H.; Music, the beautiful disturber; whether it's Bach , Beatles, 'The Boss,' blues or ballads, chances are that music speaks to your emotions, and it's no accident, *Psychology Today*; December 1, 1985

17   1999 "Please Hold" Not Always Music To Your Ears, UC Researcher Finds; University Of Cincinnati; February 25, 1999

18   Wrottesley, Catriona; *Daily Record* (Glasgow, Scotland); September 6, 2000

19   *Journal of Music Therapy* 30 (1993): 194-209

20   Hirt, Edward R., Devers, Erin E., McCrea, Sean M., I Want to Be Creative: Exploring the Role of Hedonic Contingency Theory in the Positive Mood – Cognitive Flexibility Link, *Journal of Personality and Social Psychology*, Vol. 94, No. 2, 214-230, 2008. http://www.indiana.edu/~iunews/Hirt.pdf

21   *BBC News Online;* May 26, 2003

22   *International Journal of Nursing Education Scholarship*: Vol. 1 : Iss. 1, Article 12. 2004

23   Rosenfeld, Anne H, *Psychology Today*; December 1, 1985

24   Research: Drivers Listening To Heavy Metal Twice As Likely To Go Through Red Light, *Country Evening Telegraph*, 2005, http://www.blistering.com/fastpage/fpengine.php/link/1/templateid/9783

25   Fast beat music poses a safety hazard, *Western Mail* (Cardiff, Wales); March 16, 2002

26   Brian C. Matesic, Fred Cromartie, Ed. D., United States Sports Academy; Effects Music Has On Lap Pace, Heart Rate, And Perceived Exertion Rate During a 20-minute Self-paced Run, February, 2002

27   Fauber, John, University study finds upbeat songs set pace for better workout: Knight Ridder/Tribune News Service, November 2, 2003

28   Music Increases Sporting Performance Levels By Up To 20 per cent ; Brunel University news release, October 21, 2005

29   *Medicine & Science in Sports & Exercise.* 36(5) Supplement: S126, May 2004, Volume 35(5) Supplement 1 p S286, May 2003

30   Fauber, John,, University study finds upbeat songs set pace for better workout; Knight Ridder/Tribune News Service November 2, 2003

31   Obesity may push U.S. health costs above Europe: study, Reuters, October 2, 2007

32   Obesity Bad for Brain, Study Finds. PreventDisease.com, http://preventdisease.com/news/articles/obesity_bad_for_brain_study_finds.shtml

33   Walking to the Beat, Fairleigh Dickinson University, http://inside.fdu.edu/prpt/capuano.html

34   Dancing video game helps kids avoid weight gain; Reuters, February 1, 2007

35   American Heart Association; Heart failure patients can waltz their way to healthier hearts, November 12, 2006, www.americanheart.org/presenter.jhtml?identifier=3043386

36   Matt Bean & Lisa Jones, Edited by: Jamie Bellavance; Her Sex Secrets Revealed, MensHealth.com, http://www.menshealth.com/cda/article.do?site=MensHealth&channel=sex.relationships&category=better.sex&conitem=e20b8b58d142a010VgnVCM100000cfe793cd____

37   Listening to music found to lower blood pressure, *Scientific American*/Reuters Health, May 16, 2008

38   Davis, Jeanie Lerche America, It's Time for Your Nap, WebMD, 2004

39   Mosher, Dave, Naps May Boost Memory, LiveScience.com, January 7, 2008, http://www.livescience.com/health/080107-90-minute-nap.html

40   Bower, B., Midday nap may awaken learning potential, *Science News*; June 1, 2002

41   Tanner, Lindsey, Study: On-The-Job naps might help heart, AP Medical Writer, February 12, 2007

42   www.heartmath.org/ihm-action/press-room/press-releases/coincidence-or-intuition.html

43   Ap Dijksterhuis,* Maarten W. Bos, Loran F. Nordgren, Rick B. van Baaren, On Making the Right Choice: The Deliberation-Without-Attention Effect; *Science* 17 February 2006: Vol. 311. no. 5763, pp. 1005 – 1007

44   Music improves sleep quality in older adults, Taiwanese and Case nursing researchers find; Case Western Reserve University; April 22, 2004

45   Lack of Sleep May Lead to Excess Weight; The North American Association for the Study of Obesity; November 16, 2004

46   Lack of sleep alters hormones, metabolism, simulates effects of aging; The University of Chicago Medical Center; October 21, 1999

47   Kids who get less sleep weigh more, study finds; Reuters, February 7, 2007

48   EE Epel, AE Moyer, CD Martin, S Macary, N Cummings, J Rodin and M Rebuffe-Scrive, Stress-induced cortisol, mood, and fat distribution in men; *Obesity Research* 7: 9-15, 1999

49   *Daily Record* (Glasgow, Scotland); July 27, 2001

50   *Monitor on Psychology*; Volume 31, No. 7, July/August 2000

51   Erik J. Giltay, MD, PhD; Johanna M. Geleijnse, PhD; Frans G. Zitman, MD, PhD; Tiny Hoekstra, PhD; Evert G. Schouten, MD, PhD, Dispositional Optimism and All-Cause and Cardiovascular Mortality in a Prospective Cohort of Elderly Dutch Men and Women; *Archives of General Psychiatry*; Vol. 61 No. 11, November 2004

52   Pouliot, Janine S. The Power of Music,; *World &I*; May 1, 1998

53   Menezes, Bridget, Positive attitude helps healing process; *New Straits Times*; December 27, 2003

54   Renee Montagne, *Morning Edition* (NPR); July 29, 2002

55   Rynk, Peggy, *Vibrant Life*; March 1, 2003

56   Foley, Denise, *USA Today* (Magazine); September 1, 1998

57   *Business Wire*; June 9, 2003

58   Stout, Gene, A mellower Mellencamp muses about making music; *Seattle Post-Intelligencer*; May 14, 1999

59   McCormack, Marj, *What They Don't Teach You In The Harvard Business School*; Bantam books; October 1, 1990

60   Milling, Marla Hardee, Journal Writing: A Prescription for Good Health; ThirdAge.com, http://www.thirdage.com/ebsco/files/14217.html

61   Dare to dream; *Geographical*; May 1, 2003

62   3 Climbers Die While Descending Everest; *The Associated Press.* Beijng May 23, 2006

63   Gilley, K. Matthew; Olson, Bradley J.; Walters, Bruce A., Top management team risk taking propensities and firm performance: direct and moderating effects; *Journal of Business Strategies*, September 22, 2002

64   Americans' Circle of Friends Is Shrinking, The American Sociological Association; *ASA News*; June 16, 2006